Current
CONTROVERSIES

The Energy Industry

D0366418

Other Books in the Current Controversies Series

The Energy Industry

Kristina Lyn Heitkamp, Book Editor

GREENHAVEN

PUBLISHING

Published in 2019 by Greenhaven Publishing, LLC
353 3rd Avenue, Suite 255, New York, NY 10010

Copyright © 2019 by Greenhaven Publishing, LLC

First Edition

Articles in Greenhaven Publishing anthologies are often edited for length to meet page
requirements. In addition, original titles of these works are changed to clearly present
the main thesis and to explicitly indicate the author's opinion. Every effort is made to
ensure that Greenhaven Publishing accurately reflects the original intent of the authors.
Every effort has been made to trace the owners of the copyrighted material.

Cover image: Christopher Halloran / Shutterstock.com

Library of Congress Cataloging-in-Publication Data

Names: Heitkamp, Kristina Lyn, editor.
Title: The energy industry / edited by Kristina Lyn Heitkamp.
Description: New York : Greenhaven Publishing, 2019. | Series: Current controversies |
  Includes bibliographical references and index. | Audience: Grades 9-12.
Identifiers: LCCN ISBN 9781534503014 (library bound) | ISBN 9781534503021 (pbk.)
Subjects: LCSH: Energy industries—Juvenile literature. | Power resources—Juvenile
  literature. | Renewable energy sources—Juvenile literature. | Sustainable engineering—
  Juvenile literature.
Classification: LCC TJ163.23 E547 2019 | DDC 333.79—dc23

Manufactured in the United States of America

Website: http://greenhavenpublishing.com

Contents

Chapter 1: Should Renewable Energies Replace Fossil Fuels?

Toni Pyke

As the global population steadily grows, energy consumption will likely follow. How to feed the need for energy is complex. Fossil fuels and renewable energy battle over which is the best contender for supplying future energy needs.

Yes: Renewable Energies Improve Our Health, Environment, and the Economy

Union of Concerned Scientists

Fossil fuels ravage the atmosphere, choke air and water quality, and waste natural resources. Renewable energies, on the other hand, offer a path to improved public health and several potential economic benefits.

Organisation for Economic Co-operation and Development

Our dependence on fossil fuels is powering up climate change, but a low-carbon economy is achievable with policy changes. Removing fossil fuels subsidies and barriers against renewable energy investment are both steps in the right direction.

Peter Erickson, Varun Sivaram

The study presented in this viewpoint examines how removing federal tax subsidies for oil industries would not only be good for taxpayers, but also help fight climate change. However, an energy expert disagrees and says that removing tax breaks would do nothing toward emissions reductions.

industrial emissions. This viewpoint highlights carbon-capture and storage projects in operation or under construction around the world.

No: Coal Is Still Dirty and It Is Yesterday's Energy Source

Chapter 3: Is Nuclear Power the Energy Solution to Climate Change?

Yes: Nuclear Power Is Essential to Combating Climate Change

Luis Echavarri

The population and energy consumption are expected to increase in the future. Nuclear power can help feed the need without major carbon emissions. Greenhouse gas emissions from building and producing nuclear power are comparable to those of the renewable energy industry.

The International Atomic Energy Agency

Climate change is the world's most pressing problem. Nuclear energy can help navigate toward a solution. This viewpoint highlights nuclear energy's potential to deliver large amounts of energy while reducing greenhouse gas emissions.

The Nuclear Energy Agency

As the world warms, nuclear power offers a nearly carbon-free energy. This viewpoint answers questions about nuclear energy, such as whether uranium supplies are enough to power our demand and whether radioactive waste can be safely managed.

No: Nuclear Energy Is Not a Silver Bullet Solution

Union of Concerned Scientists

While proponents of nuclear power tout it as a clean energy source, the process of sorting nuclear waste is dangerous, dirty, and expensive. This viewpoint reveals the dangerous side of nuclear power, including the risk of nuclear terrorism.

Jim Green

Producing enough nuclear power to energize the world would be extremely costly and it would take years to build new facilities to generate the energy needed. Furthermore, nuclear plants are vulnerable to climate change and weapons proliferation.

Chapter 4: Is Hydraulic Fracturing, or Fracking, Safe for Humans and the Environment?

Yes: Fracking Is Safer and Cleaner than Coal

Foreword

The word "controversy" has an undeniably unpleasant connotation. It carries a definite negative charge. Controversy can spoil family gatherings, spread a chill around classroom and campus discussion, inflame public discourse, open raw civic wounds, and lead to the ouster of public officials. We often feel that controversy is almost akin to bad manners, a rude and shocking eruption of that which must not be spoken or thought of in polite, tightly guarded society. To avoid controversy, to quell controversy, is often seen as a public good, a victory for etiquette, perhaps even a moral or ethical imperative.

Yet the studious, deliberate avoidance of controversy is also a whitewashing, a denial, a death threat to democracy. It is a false sterilizing and sanitizing and superficial ordering of the messy, ragged, chaotic, at times ugly processes by which a healthy democracy identifies and confronts challenges, engages in passionate debate about appropriate approaches and solutions, and arrives at something like a consensus and a broadly accepted and supported way forward. Controversy is the megaphone, the speaker's corner, the public square through which the citizenry finds and uses its voice. Controversy is the life's blood of our democracy and absolutely essential to the vibrant health of our society.

Our present age is certainly no stranger to controversy. We are consumed by fierce debates about technology, privacy, political correctness, poverty, violence, crime and policing, guns, immigration, civil and human rights, terrorism, militarism, environmental protection, and gender and racial equality. Loudly competing voices are raised every day, shouting opposing opinions, putting forth competing agendas, and summoning starkly different visions of a utopian or dystopian future. Often these voices attempt to shout the others down; there is precious little listening and considering among the cacophonous din. Yet listening and considering, too, are essential to the health of a democracy. If controversy is democracy's lusty lifeblood, respectful listening and careful thought are its higher faculties, its brain, its conscience.

Current Controversies does not shy away from or attempt to hush the loudly competing voices. It seeks to provide readers with as wide and representative as possible a range of articulate voices on any given controversy of the day, separates each one out to allow it to be heard clearly and fairly, and encourages careful listening to each of these well-crafted, thoughtfully expressed opinions, supplied by some of today's leading academics, thinkers, analysts, politicians, policy makers, economists, activists, change agents, and advocates. Only after listening to a wide range of opinions on an issue, evaluating the strengths and weaknesses of each argument, assessing how well the facts and available evidence mesh with the stated opinions and conclusions, and thoughtfully and critically examining one's own beliefs and conscience can the reader begin to arrive at his or her own conclusions and articulate his or her own stance on the spotlighted controversy.

This process is facilitated and supported in each Current Controversies volume by an introduction and chapter overviews that provide readers with the essential context they need to begin engaging with the spotlighted controversies, with the debates surrounding them, and with their own perhaps shifting or nascent opinions on them. Chapters are organized around several key questions that are answered with diverse opinions representing all points on the political spectrum. In its content, organization, and methodology, readers are encouraged to determine the authors' point of view and purpose, interrogate and analyze the various arguments and their rhetoric and structure, evaluate the arguments' strengths and weaknesses, test their claims against available facts and evidence, judge the validity of the reasoning, and bring into clearer, sharper focus the reader's own beliefs and conclusions and how they may differ from or align with those in the collection or those of classmates.

Research has shown that reading comprehension skills improve dramatically when students are provided with compelling, intriguing, and relevant "discussable" texts. The subject matter of these collections could not be more compelling, intriguing, or urgently relevant to today's students and the world they are poised to inherit. The anthologized articles also provide the basis for stimulating, lively, and passionate classroom debates. Students who are compelled to anticipate objections to their own argument and identify the flaws in those of an opponent read more carefully, think more critically, and steep themselves in relevant context, facts, and information more thoroughly. In short, using discussable text of the kind provided by every single volume in the Current Controversies series encourages close reading, facilitates reading comprehension, fosters research, strengthens critical thinking, and greatly enlivens and energizes classroom discussion and participation. The entire learning process is deepened, extended, and strengthened.

If we are to foster a knowledgeable, responsible, active, and engaged citizenry, we must provide readers with the intellectual, interpretive, and critical-thinking tools and experience necessary to make sense of the world around them and of the all-important debates and arguments that inform it. We must encourage them not to run away from or attempt to quell controversy but to embrace it in a responsible, conscientious, and thoughtful way, to sharpen and strengthen their own informed opinions by listening to and critically analyzing those of others. This series encourages respectful engagement with an analysis of current controversies and competing opinions and fosters a resulting increase in the strength and rigor of one's own opinions and stances. As such, it helps readers assume their rightful place in the public square and provides them with the skills necessary to uphold their awesome responsibility—guaranteeing the continued and future health of a vital, vibrant, and free democracy.

Introduction

> *First rule of oil—addicts never tell*
> *the truth to their pushers. We are*
> *the addicts, the oil producers are the*
> *pushers—we've never had an honest*
> *conversation with the Saudis.[1]*
>
> —*Thomas Friedman,*
> *American journalist*
> *and author*

Modern life is powered by energy. From filling up a fuel tank to flipping on a television, Americans have a serious energy addiction. According to the US Energy Information Administration (EIA), in 2016 the average annual energy consumption for a residential utility customer was nearly 11,000 kilowatt-hours (kWh). A kilowatt-hour is a measurement of energy. One kilowatt hour is equivalent to using a 100-watt light bulb for 10 hours, or playing a 70-watt stereo for 14 hours. It takes about one pound of coal to generate one kilowatt hour of electricity.

Estimates from EIA's *Annual Energy Outlook 2017* show that just flipping on a light switch accounted for 10 percent of both residential and commercial consumption. Using appliances such as washers and dryers, dishwashers, and computers took a bigger piece of the energy pie at 40 percent. Refrigeration was the largest single use of electricity in the commercial sector, but operating machinery accounted for nearly half the electricity consumption of manufacturers. In 2016, Louisiana consumed the most electricity per customer, while Hawaii consumed the least.

The energy industry includes the companies extracting and distributing the fuel as well as the consumers who guzzle the fuel. Energy consumption can be broken down into five major sources: petroleum, natural gas, coal, nuclear power, and renewable energy. Nonrenewable sources, such as coal and natural gas, cannot easily be replenished. Fossil fuels are extracted from the earth in the form of a liquid, gas, or solid. Natural gas, coal, and crude oil are all fossil fuels, which means the energy source was formed from the fossils of animals and plants that lived millions of years ago. Crude oil is used to make petroleum products, such as gasoline for vehicles. Fossil fuels are a finite source, and not renewable. Once they're used up, they're gone.

However, renewable energy sources can be naturally replenished and will never run out. There are five main renewable energy sources: solar, wind, geothermal, biomass, and hydropower. According to EIA, in 2016 about 10 percent of total US energy consumption was from renewable energy sources. Using renewable energies to feed our energy need helps to reduce greenhouse gas emissions and the air pollution associated with fossil fuel production. Renewable energy has the potential to mitigate human-caused climate change and provide a low environmental and human impact. Yet critics of renewable energy confront the amount of land and water used to produce large-scale power, claiming it's just not a realistic option. Additionally, it would be costly and difficult to transition the current energy system to accommodate renewable energy.

Energy consumption in the United States is expected to continue growing. According to the EIA, electricity use in the United States in 2016 was more than thirteen times greater than in 1950. Energy consumption is projected to increase 56 percent by the year 2040. Most energy experts agree that energy use will skyrocket, but there is great controversy on how the industry should provide service. Nuclear power and renewable energy are the world's fastest growing energy sources, but fossil fuels such as coal and natural gas continue to supply over 80 percent of energy use.

When considering the future of energy use and selecting a source with the capabilities to satiate America's voracious energy appetite, several variables are debated. Points of contention include energy security, energy safety, and the environmental and human impacts of energy.

Keep it local. Procuring energy sources locally secures energy independence. If the United States is self-sufficient in oil and gas production, the ups and downs of the global market may not impact the country. Plus, investing in local energy production provides jobs and local economy growth.

Keep it safe. Maintaining health and safety standards in the extraction of energy can also be a source of contention. Uranium mining to generate nuclear energy may be considered safe, but radioactive waste storage and disposal is problematic and dangerous. Fracking is another energy operation that is riddled with safety concerns. Fracking waste contaminates drinking water supplies, and some scientists propose that fracking operations may cause earthquakes.

Keep it clean. Coal is cheap to produce and found locally, but producing and using coal has damaging effects on air and water quality. Additionally, emissions from burning coal contribute to human-caused climate change.

The controversy over the energy industry involves many players, from energy economists debating the financial costs of transitioning to renewables to engineers testing carbon-capture technologies and uses for the stored carbon from clean coal. Dr. Robert Kirkman tackles the environmental ethics of scientists and engineers researching risks of hydraulic fracturing, or fracking. On the other hand, energy economist Jacquelyn Pless says if fracking is done right, the risks are lowered. The viewpoints in *Current Controversies: The Energy Industry* will help readers navigate the different voices in the debate, and may encourage a deeper understanding in personal energy consumption.

Notes
1. "The oil and gas industry," by B.R., Sep 28th 2012, *The Economist.*

CHAPTER 1

Should Renewable Energies Replace Fossil Fuels?

The Energy Debate: Fossil Fuels Versus Renewable Energy

Toni Pyke

Toni Pyke is a part-time researcher and writer with developmenteducation.ie based in Kampala, Uganda. She recently completed her doctoral research on men and masculinities in southern Africa.

Fossil Fuels (coal, oil, petroleum, and natural gas) are originally formed from plants and animals that lived hundreds of millions of years ago and became buried deep beneath the Earth's surface. These then collectively transformed into the combustible materials that we use today for fuel. The earliest known fossil fuel deposits are from about 500 million years ago, when most of the major groups of animals first appeared on Earth. The later fossil fuels, such as peat or lignite coal (soft coal), began forming from about five million years ago.

Currently, we are (over)dependent on fossil fuels to heat our homes, run our cars, power our offices, industry and manufacturing, and respond to our insatiable desire to power all of our electrical goods. Nearly all of the energy needed to meet our demands—80 percent of global energy—comes from burning fossil fuels. At the current rate of global energy demands, fossil fuels cannot replenish fast enough to meet these growing needs. The (over)consumption of these non-renewable fuels has been linked to the emission of greenhouse gases and pollutants into the atmosphere—the leading cause of global warming and climate change.

In Ireland, for example, our energy consumption from fossil fuels was 89% in 2013. Our highest demand for fossil fuel energy over the last 51 years was experienced during the period of high growth under the 'Celtic Tiger' (2004), where we required 93.39%. The lowest energy consumption value (67.24%) was in 1960, more than half a century ago! Ireland is ranked 46th out of 136 countries in its fossil fuel energy consumption. That's higher than the UK (52nd) and the US (56th)!

Renewables

Renewable energy is energy that is derived from natural processes (e.g. sunlight and wind). Solar, wind, geothermal, hydropower, bioenergy and ocean power are sources of renewable energy. Currently, renewables are utilised in the electricity, heating and cooling and transport sectors. Renewable energy, collectively provides only about 7 percent of the world's energy needs. This means that fossil fuels, along with nuclear energy—a non-renewable energy source—are supplying 93% of the world's energy resources. Nuclear energy (a controversial energy source among public opinion) currently provides 6% of the world's energy supplies.

The Issues

Burning fossil fuels creates carbon dioxide, the main greenhouse gas emitter that contributes to global warming, which hit its peak in 2012. In the last 30 years, temperatures have risen to the warmest since records began. If we continue to pump greenhouse gases into our environment the average global temperature could increase by 1°C to 4°C by 2100. Even if we changed today to using more renewable resources instead of fossil fuels for example, increases could be between 1 to 2.5°C.

The 20th century saw the most prolific population growth and industrial development, which was and remains totally dependent on the use of fossil fuel for energy.

Estimates for fossil fuel reserves depletion range from between 50-120 years. None of these projections are very appealing for a global community that is so heavily dependent on energy to meet even our basic human needs—needs that keep growing.

Predictions estimate that global energy demand will grow by a third by 2035. Also critical to consider is the more than 1.2 *billion* people around the world who still do not have access—yet—to electricity. As the global population continues to grow—predicted to be nine billion people over the next 50 years—the world's energy demands will increase proportionately.

Scientists maintain that the impact of global warming on the environment is widespread. In the Arctic and Antarctica, warmer temperatures are melting ice, which leads to increases in sea levels and alters the composition of the surrounding sea water. Rising sea levels impacts on settlements, agriculture and fishing both commercially and recreationally. Air pollution is also a direct result of the use of fossil fuels, resulting in smog, and the degradation of human health and plant growth. There is the negative impact on natural ecosystems that result from collecting fossil fuels, particularly coal and oil. There is also the continuing threat of oil spills that devastate ecosystems and the impact of mining on land vitality.

The Future

The discussions around climate change and energy problems today centre around the potential for technical solutions to energy demands that are *cost effective*. So far, the alternative to fossil fuels has been around renewable energy sources, which are expected to play an increasingly vital role in the mix of power generation over the next century. The demands on these alternative energy sources are inordinate—they will need to not only keep up with the increasing population growth, but needs to go beyond these demands by contributing to the replacement of fossil fuel energy production in order to meet future energy needs and consider the natural environment.

However, the argument from governments, oil, coal and natural gas companies is that until renewable energy sources become more viable as major energy providers, the only alternative in meeting the increasing demands for energy from a growing global population that requires more and more energy, is to continue to extract fossil fuel reserves.

The Debate

Agree 1: Switching to Renewable Energy Is Not as Simple as It Is Being Made Out to Be

"It is commonly assumed that greenhouse gas and energy problems can be solved by switching from fossil fuel sources of energy to renewables. However, little attention has been given to exploring the limits to renewable energy. Unfortunately, people working on renewable energy technologies tend not to throw critical light on the difficulties and limits. They typically make enthusiastic claims regarding the potential of their specific technologies." (Alex Epstein)

The idea of drawing our energy from sources that are renewable, independent of foreign nations, and do not emit greenhouse gases has powerful appeal. But capturing these resources is expensive, and many are intermittent, which complicates using them on a large scale. Furthermore, it takes time and money to change distribution and consumption of energy, meaning we will be dependent on fossil fuels until we can afford this switch. Finally, bringing new renewable energy technologies to market causes problems both in regard to cost and convenience, meaning a switch from fossil fuels to renewable energy is not a simple task.

Disagree 1: Leaving Fossil Fuels in the Ground Is Good for Everyone

"To deliver a 50% probability (which is not exactly reassuring) of no more than 2C of warming this century, the world would have to leave two-thirds of its fossil fuel reserves unexploited. I should point out that reserves are just a small fraction of resources (which means all the minerals in the Earth's crust). The reserve is that proportion of a mineral resource which has been discovered, quantified and is viable to exploit in current conditions: in other words that's good

to go.... a third of the world's oil reserves, half its gas reserves and 80% of its coal reserves must be left untouched to avert extremely dangerous levels of global warming. 2C is dangerous enough; at present we are on course for around 5C by the time the century ends, with no obvious end in sight beyond 2100." (George Monbiot, *The Guardian*, 2015)

Fossil fuels are not renewable, they can't be made again. Once they are gone, they're gone.

Agree 2: Renewables Cannot Provide the Required Amount of Energy to Supply Demand (Intermittency)

Solar and wind technology, after 50 years of subsidies, produces less than 1 percent of the world's energy—and, because the sun and wind provide only intermittent energy, continue to require fossil fuel backups.

The issue of intermittency from solar and wind means that is difficult to get reliable power from either as it is weather dependent—which, particularly in Ireland is unpredictable. This creates a need for energy storage (which is currently not efficient enough to be cost effective) or needs traditional fossil fuels or nuclear power to supplement.

"As you look at the jagged and woefully insufficient bursts of electricity from solar and wind, remember this: some reliable source of energy needed to do the heavy lifting. In the case of Germany, much of that energy is coal. As Germany has paid tens of billions of dollars to subsidize solar panels and windmills, fossil fuel capacity, especially coal, has not been shut down—it has increased. Why? Because Germans need more energy, and they cannot rely on the renewables." (Alex Epstein)

"It is concluded that although the foregoing figures are not precise or confident, their magnitudes indicate that it will not be possible to meet a 1000 EJ/yr energy target for 2050 from alternative energy sources, within safe greenhouse gas emission levels ... Such a goal could not be achieved without radical change in social, economic, political and cultural systems." (Ted Trainer)

Much of the debate around renewables is in reference to the 'present' energy demands, where the anticipated demand for energy in the future is expected to double by 2050. "The crucial question is can renewables meet the future demand for energy in a society that is fiercely and blindly committed to limitless increases in "living standards" and economic output. The absurdity of this commitment is easily shown. If 9 billion people were to rise to the "living standards" we in rich countries will have in 2070 given 3% p.a. economic growth, then total world economic output would be 60 times as great as it is now! It is concluded that the investment cost that would be involved in deriving total world energy supply from renewable sources would be unaffordable. Full dependence on renewable energy can only be done if we move to lifestyles and systems that require only a small fraction of the present rich world per capita energy consumption.

Renewables could provide around of 25% of energy needs in some countries, but much of the generating capacity would have to be duplicated in the form of fossil or nuclear plant for use when there is little sun or wind; and the amount of coal use that will continue to be required would continue to exceed safe greenhouse gas emission limits.

Disagree 2: Renewable Energy Can Meet Energy Needs in a Safe and Reliable Way

"…*The key is to have a mix of sources spread over a wide area: solar and wind power, biogas, biomass and geothermal sources. In the future, ocean energy can contribute. Intelligent technologies can track and manage energy use patterns, provide flexible power that follows demand through the day, use better storage options and group producers together to form virtual power plants. With all these solutions we can secure the renewable energy future needed. We just need smart grids to put it all together and effectively 'keep the lights on.'*" (Greenpeace.org 2014)

Continued research has made renewable energy more affordable today than 25 years ago. The cost of wind energy has declined from 40 cents per kilowatt-hour to less than 5 cents. The cost of electricity from the sun, through photovoltaics (literally meaning "light-electricity") has dropped from more than \$1/kilowatt-hour in 1980 to nearly 20cents/kilowatt-hour today. And ethanol fuel costs have plummeted from \$4 per gallon in the early 1980s to \$1.20 today.

The amount of energy used in Irish homes has decreased by 32 per cent since 1990 despite a 50 per cent increase in the average floor area of residential properties. Renewable energy last year accounted for 21% of the amount used in the electricity sector, 5.7% of the amount used for heat and 4.9 per cent of that used in transport.

By 2050 almost all of global energy needs can be met with renewable energy share: 41 percent by 2030 and 82 percent by 2050. That would be the global electricity supply—energy used in buildings and industry would come from renewable energy sources. The transport sector, in particular aviation and shipping, would be the last sector to become fossil fuel free.

[...]

Emerging economies do not need to go down a path of relying on fossil fuels. Just as many developing countries skipped land lines and went straight to cellular telephones, these countries can leapfrog right to affordable clean energy. Many have already taken advantage of the benefits of renewable energy and recognised the long-term benefits. For example, in Uganda less than 15% of a total population of 38 million people, have access to electricity. The majority of the population is dependent on kerosene or charcoal for their energy and light, both of which are expensive and environmentally damaging. Yet, the population is embracing the potential for clean energy alternatives being promoted within the country.

Intermittency is an issue at the moment as the technology is expanding, but it can be managed by thinking about the overall energy system. Over reliance on one renewable technology could result both in massive variability in output over short time periods and in severe risk of big gaps in generation.

The way round this is:

a) a dispersed portfolio of generation connected by a wide grid and

b) clean gas on standby

Disagree 3: Fossil Fuel Energy Costs Do
Not Factor In all the 'Hidden' Costs

"*Investing in clean energy is not only good for the economic growth, it is good for people. The unfortunate reality is that those in the poorest countries are often the most vulnerable to climate change—whether from rising seas that threaten homes and water supplies or droughts that drive up food prices. This is the human cost of fossil fuels that often goes unmentioned in balance sheets and gross domestic product statistics.*"

If the full cost of fossil fuel generation (including climate impact) were included then the costs would be comparable.

[…]

The costs of some renewable energy inputs such as Photovoltaic solar panels have halved in price since 2008 and the capital cost of a solar-power plant—of which panels account for slightly under half—fell by 22 percent between 2010 and 2013. In a few sunny places, solar power is providing electricity to the grid as cheaply as conventional coal- or gas-fired power plants.

As the large utilities' fossil and nuclear plants become more expensive and alternatives become cheaper, savvy consumers are looking to decrease their dependence on the utilities' power supply. To cope, the utilities are trying to decouple their increasing costs from the amount of electricity they sell, further increasing the cost advantages of renewables and other alternatives. Renewables, with zero-marginal-costs, helped push down wholesale prices to 8-year lows in 2013.

[…]

Agree 4: Renewable Energy Utilises Too Much Land, Meaning Problems in Scalability and Storage

A problem with solar and wind energy is the sheer scale of land that is required to obtain as much energy as even a small coal fire power plant can produce. Storing renewable energy more effectively and inexpensive energy from wind or solar could become much more viable than they are currently. However right now, no cost effective forms of energy storage exist, and are not foreseen.

Very large scale production of renewable energy, especially via solar thermal and PV farms located at the most favourable regions, will involve long distance transmission. European supply from solar thermal fields will probably have to be via several thousand kilometre long HVDC (high-voltage, direct current) lines from North Africa and the Middle East. Expected power losses from long distance plus local distribution are predicted to be around 15 percent. This makes it different than coal, natural gas, and nuclear, and in some senses worse. It means that it can't supply 100 percent of our needs, and intermittency needs to be factored into any electricity system design. An intelligently designed energy system using very basic "smart grid" technology could support easily up to 25 percent production from intermittent renewables without significant strain on resources.

[...]

The Benefits of Renewable Energies Far Outweigh Fossil Fuels

Union of Concerned Scientists

The Union of Concerned Scientists puts rigorous, independent science to work to solve our planet's most pressing problems.

Wind turbines and solar panels are an increasingly common sight. But why? What are the benefits of renewable energies—and how do they improve our health, environment, and economy?

Less Global Warming

Human activity is overloading our atmosphere with carbon dioxide and other global warming emissions. These gases act like a blanket, trapping heat. The result is a web of significant and harmful impacts, from stronger, more frequent storms, to drought, sea level rise, and extinction.

In the United States, about 29 percent of global warming emissions come from our electricity sector. Most of those emissions come from fossil fuels like coal and natural gas.

In contrast, most renewable energy sources produce little to no global warming emissions. Even when including "life cycle" emissions of clean energy (i.e., the emissions from each stage of a technology's life—manufacturing, installation, operation, decommissioning), the global warming emissions associated with renewable energy are minimal.

The comparison becomes clear when you look at the numbers. Burning natural gas for electricity releases between 0.6 and 2 pounds of carbon dioxide equivalent per kilowatt-hour (CO_2E/kWh); coal emits between 1.4 and 3.6 pounds of CO_2E/kWh. Wind, on the

"Benefits of Renewable Energy Use," Union of Concerned Scientists, April 8, 2013. http://www.ucsusa.org/clean-energy/renewable-energy/public-benefits-of-renewable-power#.Wflow9KWa1s. Reprinted by permission.

other hand, is responsible for only 0.02 to 0.04 pounds of $CO_2E/$ kWh on a life-cycle basis; solar 0.07 to 0.2; geothermal 0.1 to 0.2; and hydroelectric between 0.1 and 0.5.

Renewable electricity generation from biomass can have a wide range of global warming emissions depending on the resource and whether or not it is sustainably sourced and harvested.

Increasing the supply of renewable energy would allow us to replace carbon-intensive energy sources and significantly reduce US global warming emissions.

For example, a 2009 UCS analysis found that a 25 percent by 2025 national renewable electricity standard would lower power plant CO_2 emissions 277 million metric tons annually by 2025— the equivalent of the annual output from 70 typical (600 MW) new coal plants.

In addition, a ground-breaking study by the US Department of Energy's National Renewable Energy Laboratory (NREL) explored the feasibility of generating 80 percent of the country's electricity from renewable sources by 2050. They found that renewable energy could help reduce the electricity sector's emissions by approximately *81 percent.*

Improved Public Health

The air and water pollution emitted by coal and natural gas plants is linked with breathing problems, neurological damage, heart attacks, cancer, premature death, and a host of other serious problems. The pollution affects everyone: one Harvard University study estimated the life cycle costs and public health effects of coal to be an estimated $74.6 billion every year. That's equivalent to 4.36 cents per kilowatt-hour of electricity produced—about one-third of the average electricity rate for a typical US home.

Most of these negative health impacts come from air and water pollution that clean energy technologies simply don't produce. Wind, solar, and hydroelectric systems generate electricity with no associated air pollution emissions. Geothermal and biomass systems emit *some* air pollutants, though total air emissions are generally much lower than those of coal- and natural gas-fired power plants.

In addition, wind and solar energy require essentially no water to operate and thus do not pollute water resources or strain supplies by competing with agriculture, drinking water, or other important water needs. In contrast, fossil fuels can have a significant impact on water resources: both coal mining and natural gas drilling can pollute sources of drinking water, and all thermal power plants, including those powered by coal, gas, and oil, withdraw and consume water for cooling.

Biomass and geothermal power plants, like coal- and natural gas-fired power plants, may require water for cooling. Hydroelectric power plants can disrupt river ecosystems both upstream and downstream from the dam. However, NREL's 80-percent-by-2050 renewable energy study, which included biomass and geothermal, found that total water consumption and withdrawal would decrease significantly in a future with high renewables.

Inexhaustible Energy

Strong winds, sunny skies, abundant plant matter, heat from the earth, and fast-moving water can each provide a vast and constantly replenished supply of energy. A relatively small fraction of US electricity currently comes from these sources, but that could change: studies have repeatedly shown that renewable energy can provide a significant share of future electricity needs, even after accounting for potential constraints.

In fact, a major government-sponsored study found that clean energy could contribute somewhere between three and 80 times its 2013 levels, depending on assumptions. And the previously mentioned NREL study found that renewable energy could comfortably provide up to 80 percent of US electricity by 2050.

Jobs and Other Economic Benefits

Compared with fossil fuel technologies, which are typically mechanized and capital intensive, the renewable energy industry is more labor intensive. Solar panels need humans to install them; wind farms need technicians for maintenance.

This means that, on average, more jobs are created for each unit of electricity generated from renewable sources than from fossil fuels.

Renewable energy already supports thousands of jobs in the United States. In 2016, the wind energy industry directly employed over 100,000 full-time-equivalent employees in a variety of capacities, including manufacturing, project development, construction and turbine installation, operations and maintenance, transportation and logistics, and financial, legal, and consulting services. More than 500 factories in the United States manufacture parts for wind turbines, and wind power project installations in 2016 alone represented $13.0 billion in investments.

Other renewable energy technologies employ even more workers. In 2016, the solar industry employed more than 260,000 people, including jobs in solar installation, manufacturing, and sales, a 25% increase over 2015. The hydroelectric power industry employed approximately 66,000 people in 2017; the geothermal industry employed 5,800 people.

Increased support for renewable energy could create even more jobs. The 2009 Union of Concerned Scientists study of a 25-percent-by-2025 renewable energy standard found that such a policy would create more than three times as many jobs (more than 200,000) as producing an equivalent amount of electricity from fossil fuels.

In contrast, the entire coal industry employed 160,000 people in 2016.

In addition to the jobs *directly* created in the renewable energy industry, growth in clean energy can create positive economic "ripple" effects. For example, industries in the renewable energy supply chain will benefit, and unrelated local businesses will benefit from increased household and business incomes.

Local governments also benefit from clean energy, most often in the form of property and income taxes and other payments from renewable energy project owners. Owners of the land on which wind projects are built often receive lease payments ranging from $3,000 to $6,000 per megawatt of installed capacity, as well as payments for power line easements and road rights-of-way. They may also earn royalties based on the project's annual revenues. Farmers and rural landowners can generate new sources of supplemental income by producing feedstocks for biomass power facilities.

UCS analysis found that a 25-by-2025 national renewable electricity standard would stimulate $263.4 billion in new capital investment for renewable energy technologies, $13.5 billion in new landowner income from biomass production and/or wind land lease payments, and $11.5 billion in new property tax revenue for local communities.

Stable Energy Prices

Renewable energy is providing affordable electricity across the country right now, and can help stabilize energy prices in the future.

Although renewable facilities require upfront investments to build, they can then operate at very low cost (for most clean energy technologies, the "fuel" is free). As a result, renewable energy prices can be very stable over time.

Moreover, the costs of renewable energy technologies have declined steadily, and are projected to drop even more. For example, the average price to install solar dropped more than 70 percent between 2010 and 2017. The cost of generating electricity from wind dropped 66 percent between 2009 and 2016. Costs will likely decline even further as markets mature and companies increasingly take advantage of economies of scale.

In contrast, fossil fuel prices can vary dramatically and are prone to substantial price swings. For example, there was a rapid increase in US coal prices due to rising global demand before 2008, then a rapid fall after 2008 when global demands declined. Likewise, natural gas prices have fluctuated greatly since 2000.

Using more renewable energy can lower the prices of and demand for natural gas and coal by increasing competition and diversifying our energy supplies. And an increased reliance on renewable energy can help protect consumers when fossil fuel prices spike.

Reliability and Resilience

Wind and solar are less prone to large-scale failure because they are distributed and modular. Distributed systems are spread out over a large geographical area, so a severe weather event in one location will not cut off power to an entire region. Modular systems are composed of numerous individual wind turbines or solar arrays. Even if some of the equipment in the system is damaged, the rest can typically continue to operate.

For example, Hurricane Sandy damaged fossil fuel-dominated electric generation and distribution systems in New York and New Jersey and left millions of people without power. In contrast, renewable energy projects in the Northeast weathered Hurricane Sandy with minimal damage or disruption.

Water scarcity is another risk for non-renewable power plants. Coal, nuclear, and many natural gas plants depend on having sufficient water for cooling, which means that severe droughts and heat waves can put electricity generation at risk. Wind and solar photovoltaic systems do not require water to generate electricity and can operate reliably in conditions that may otherwise require closing a fossil fuel-powered plant.

The risk of disruptive events will also increase in the future as droughts, heat waves, more intense storms, and increasingly severe wildfires become more frequent due to global warming— increasing the need for resilient, clean technologies.

Politicians Stand in the Way of a Low-Carbon Economy

Organisation for Economic Co-operation and Development

The mission of the Organisation for Economic Co-operation and Development (OECD) is to promote policies that will improve the economic and social well-being of people around the world.

To limit the impact of climate change, net greenhouse gas emissions must fall globally to zero by the end of the century. Three policy approaches are essential to meeting this goal:

- We must strengthen carbon pricing and remove fossil fuel subsidies;
- We must remove barriers to green investment; and
- We must align policies across the economy to leave fossil fuels behind as well as improve transparency on climate finance.

What's the Issue?

Fossil fuels account for around 81% of the energy we use. Despite the increasing focus on renewable sources of energy, the share of fossil fuels in the energy mix has changed little since the 1990s. But as well as supplying our energy needs, fossil fuels are also the major source of the carbon emissions that are fueling climate change.

The legacy of human activity on the planet means that some level of climate change is now inevitable. But there is still time to limit the extent of the temperature rise to under 2°C, rather than the 3 to 5°C rise we are currently facing. For this to happen, we must achieve zero net greenhouse-gas emissions globally by the end of the century.

OECD (2015), Three steps to a low-carbon economy, OECD Policy Brief, November 2015, https://www.oecd.org/policy-briefs/Three-steps-to-a-low-carbon-economy.pdf.

Reaching this goal will be challenging but by no means impossible. At the policy level it will require governments to disentangle their often contradictory approaches to climate change and energy. On the one hand, most governments are now committed to reducing carbon emissions. But, at the same time, many still subsidise fossil fuel producers and the use of coal and other fossil fuels. Many, also, are doing too little to encourage investment in alternative sources of energy and the rest of the green economy. Resolving these contradictions, and developing a genuine global partnership to fight climate change, are essential to getting to zero net emissions.

Why Is This Important?

Unless governments take concerted action, fossil fuels will remain humanity's energy source of choice, contributing still further to the build-up of greenhouse gases. Despite the urgency of the challenge, policies in many countries continue to favour fossil fuels. Take coal: it is usually the least heavily taxed of all fossil fuels and is also generally subject to very low or no import tariffs. By contrast, renewable energy sources may be subject to import tariffs of at least 10%, and in some cases as high as 30%.

Unfortunately, there is often strong resistance to reducing our reliance on fossil fuels, with critics warning of risks to economic growth and competitiveness. However, there is little evidence that many of the steps essential for the transition to a low-carbon economy—such as subsidy reform and improving energy efficiency—pose any such threats. Equally, there is a high economic cost to doing nothing: research by the OECD suggests that, by 2060, climate change could reduce global GDP by between 1% and 3.3% a year.

A second challenge is posed by the extent to which our economies and societies remain deeply entangled with fossil fuel use and exploitation. For example, many government budgets and pension funds still rely heavily on returns from the coal and oil industries. Disentangling these linkages will require clear and predictable policies that ensure the true environment cost of fossil fuels is transmitted to producers and users.

What Should Policy Makers Do?

The potential for making rapid cuts in carbon emissions is greater than many people realise. It can be made to happen if governments act quickly in three main policy areas: strengthen carbon pricing and remove fossil fuel subsidies; remove barriers to investment in the green economy; align policies across the economy—and not just in climate-related areas—and increase transparency on climate finance flows.

Strengthen Carbon Pricing and Cut Fossil Fuel Subsidies

Despite rising investment in renewables, we remain overly reliant on fossil fuels. In part, this is because the cost of fossil fuels to consumers does not reflect the environmental damage caused by these fuel sources. Equally, a range of subsidies, soft tax arrangements and investment allowances insulate producers from the true cost of extracting and using fossil fuels. While a gradually rising carbon price is necessary, there is an urgent need for governments to remove subsidies on fossil fuels to strengthen price signalling, both for producers and consumers. But with some notable exceptions, too few countries have taken action. Similarly, more needs to be done to introduce realistic carbon taxes. And while there has been progress on introducing emissions trading systems, allowance prices within these systems are generally too low.

Remove Barriers to Investing in the Green Economy

The underpricing of fossil fuels also serves as a barrier to investment in energy efficiency and renewable energy sources. For example, because the cost of pollution is not being accurately priced, fossil fuel projects appear more competitive than clean infrastructure projects. But there are other barriers to such investment. These include unpredictable policy and regulatory environments; market and regulatory arrangements that favour existing fossil fuel power generators; high financing costs; and barriers to international trade and investment, such as local-content requirements for solar and wind-energy projects. The need to tackle these policy shortcomings is urgent, especially in light of the opportunities for green investment that are opening up as existing power plants reach the end of their operating lives.

Align Policies Across the Economy and Support Climate Finance

The complex challenge of tackling climate change requires transformative domestic policies that build extensively on international trust and co-operation. Leaving fossil fuels behind implies change that will cut across every aspect of the economy. Tracking progress effectively is essential to providing a clear sense of whether or not carbon-pricing instruments and other policies to address greenhouse gas emissions are being implemented.

A major international effort is also needed to support climate change mitigation and adaptation in developing countries, many of which face particular risks from rising temperatures. Developed countries have committed to provide $100 billion a year by 2020 and have made significant progress towards meeting this goal: in 2014, climate finance reached an estimated $61.8 billion. That is encouraging, but it is also clear that a sustained effort will be needed to meet the 2020 goal.

Oil Subsidies—More Material for Climate Change

Peter Erickson, Varun Sivaram

Peter Erickson is a staff scientist at the Stockholm Environment Institute. Varun Sivaram is the acting director of Energy Security and Climate Change, Council on Foreign Relations.

As Congress moves towards tax reform, there is one industry that hasn't yet come up: oil. While subsidies for renewable energy are often in the cross-hairs of tax discussions, the billions in federal tax subsidies for the oil industry rarely are; indeed, some subsidies are nearing their 100th birthday. And yet, removing oil subsidies would be good not only for taxpayers, but for the climate as well.

The lack of attention on petroleum subsidies is not for lack of analysis. Congress' own Joint Committee on Taxation values the subsidies at more than $2 billion annually. (Other researchers have put the total much higher.) Just in the last year, two major studies have assessed in detail how these subsidies affect investment returns in the US oil industry. The two analyses—one published by the Council on Foreign Relations (CFR) and the other in *Nature Energy* (which I coauthored)—both show the majority of subsidy value goes directly to profits, not to new investment.

That inefficiency—both studies argue—is reason enough for Congress to end the subsidies to the oil industry.

But oil subsidies also have another strike against them: oil is a major contributor to climate change. The burning of gasoline, diesel, and other petroleum products is responsible for one-third of global CO_2 emissions. That climate impact is one of the reasons

"Rebuttal: Oil Subsidies—More Material for Climate Change Than You Might Think," by Peter Erickson, Senior Scientist, SEI, The Council on Foreign Relations, November 2, 2017. Reprinted by permission.

the Obama Administration had committed, with other nations in the G7, to end these subsidies by 2025.

Both the CFR and *Nature Energy* analyses arrive at a similar figure as to the net climate impact. As CFR fellow Varun Sivaram notes in a previous post on this blog comparing the two studies, the CFR study finds that subsidy removal would reduce global oil consumption by about half a percent. Our analysis for the *Nature Energy* study also finds a reduction in global oil consumption of about half a percent. (You won't find this result in our paper, but it is what our oil market model, described in the online Supplementary Information, implies.)

The most critical place where the studies—or rather, authors— differ is how they put this amount of oil in context. (Our study also addresses many more subsidies, and in much more detail, than the CFR study, but that is not the point I wish to address here.)

Sivaram refers to the half-percent decrease in global oil consumption as "measly…washed out by the ordinary volatility of oil prices and resulting changes in consumption…the nearly-undetectable change in global oil consumption means that the climate effects of US tax breaks are negligible."

I would argue that this assertion confuses the effect of subsidies on oil consumption with our ability to measure the change. But before I get into it further, let me first describe how much oil and CO_2 we are talking about.

By the CFR paper's estimates, removal of US oil subsidies would lead to a drop in global oil consumption of 300,000 to 500,000 barrels per day (corresponding to 0.3% to 0.5% of the global oil market). The sequential effects in their model are shown in the chart below, which I made based on their results. It shows their lower-end case, in which global oil consumption drops by 300,000 barrels per day (bpd). (This case is described in their paper as using EIA's reference case oil price forecast and an upward-sloping OPEC supply curve.) In their model, a drop of over 600,000 bpd in US supply from subsidy removal is partially replaced by other sources of US, OPEC, and other rest-of-world supply, yielding a net reduction in global consumption of roughly half as much (300,000 bpd, shown in the right column). (This ratio itself is also interesting and important. For each barrel of oil not developed because of subsidies, this case shows a drop in global oil consumption of 0.45 barrels. The CFR study's other three cases show a drop of 0.51, 0.63, and 0.82 barrels of global consumption for each US barrel left undeveloped.)

Each barrel of oil yields, conservatively, about 400 kg of CO_2 once burned, per IPCC figures. So, the range of impacts on oil consumption in the CFR study (again, reductions of 300-500k bpd or 110 million to 200 million bbl annually) implies a drop in global CO_2 emissions of about 40–70 million tons of CO annually. (The actual emissions decrease from subsidy removal could well be greater, because this estimate doesn't count other gases released in the course of extracting a barrel of oil, such as methane or other CO_2 from energy used on-site).

From a policy perspective, 40 to 70 million tons of CO_2 is not a trivial (measly) amount. Rather, it is comparable in scale to other US government efforts to reduce greenhouse gas emissions. For example, President Obama's Climate Action Plan contained a host of high-profile measures that, individually, would have reduced annual (domestic) greenhouse gas emissions by 5 million tons (limits on methane from oil and gas extraction on federal land), 60 million tons (efficiency standards for big trucks), and 200 million tons (efficiency standards for cars).

The CFR authors don't quantify their findings in CO_2 terms, however, and Sivaram refers to oil market volatility as a way to discount CFR's findings on reduced oil consumption, concluding that the effects are "undetectable" and "negligible." The argument is essentially that because other changes in the oil market are bigger, and can mask the independent effect of subsidy removal, that subsidy removal has no effect on climate change.

This line of argument conflates causality, scale and likelihood of impact (which in this case are either all known, or can be estimated) with ability to monitor, detect and attribute changes (which is rarely possible in any case, even for more traditional policies focused on oil consumption). By this logic, almost *any* climate policy could also be discounted as immaterial, because it is rare to be able to directly observe with confidence both the intended result of a policy and the counterfactual—what would have happened otherwise.

Rather, I would argue that if we are to meet the challenge of global climate change, we'll need these 40 to 70 million tons of avoided CO_2, and many more, even if there is uncertainty about exactly how big the impact will be. Concluding an action represents a small fraction of the climate problem is less a statement about that action than it is about the massive scale of the climate challenge. Indeed, as the Obama White House Council on Environmental Quality stated, such a comparison is "not an appropriate method for characterizing the potential impacts associated with a proposed action... because...[it] does not reveal anything beyond the nature of the climate change challenge itself."

So, I argue that subsidy removal is indeed material for the climate, even by the CFR report's own math. And as Sivaram also notes, the CO_2 emission reductions would multiply as other countries also phase out their subsidies.

Lastly, I need to disagree with Sivaram's statement that our study is "written in a misleading way." He asserts this because in the *Nature Energy* article we focus on the entire CO_2 emissions from each barrel, rather than apply an oil market economic model as described above that counts only the net, or incremental, global CO_2. But the incremental analysis method above is not the only way to describe CO_2 emissions. Indeed, comparing the possible CO_2 emissions from a particular source to the global remaining carbon budget is a simple and established way to gauge magnitudes, and nicely complements the incremental analysis enabled by oil market models.

As another noted subsidy expert—Ron Steenblik of the OECD—commented separately in *Nature Energy*, our analytical approach provides an important advance because it enables "researchers to look at the combined effect of many individual subsidies flowing to specific projects and to use project-specific data to gauge eligibility and uptake." Similar assessments of other countries, and other fossil fuels, would provide an important window on the distortionary impacts of these subsidies and their perverse impacts on global efforts to contain climate change.

Sivaram Response to Erickson Rebuttal

First of all, I am grateful to Peter Erickson for responding in this way to a blog post I wrote that was critical of his conclusions. His response was graceful and sophisticated—I think I largely agree with it, and he's pointed out some holes in my post that I want to acknowledge. However, I do still stand by my headline, "No, Tax Breaks for US Oil and Gas Companies Probably Don't Materially Affect Climate Change." In fact, I think the Erickson rebuttal above reinforces just that point.

Tackling the overall thesis first: in his rebuttal, Erickson is willing to accept that a reasonable estimate for the carbon impact of US tax breaks for oil and gas companies is 40–70 million tons of carbon dioxide emissions annually (there may be other greenhouse gas emissions, such as methane, that increase the climate impact). Erickson even compares the magnitude of this negative climate impact with the positive impact of President Obama's efficiency standards for big trucks.

I am absolutely willing to accept that removing US tax breaks for oil companies would be about as big a deal, in terms of direct emissions reduction, as setting domestic efficiency standards for big trucks. Importantly, this direct impact is trivial on a global scale, which is the point that I made in my original post, reinforcing Dr. Metcalf's conclusion in his CFR paper.

I am, however, sympathetic to Erickson's argument that the world needs a rollback of tax breaks, efficiency standards for big trucks, and a whole suite of other policies in the United States and other major economies to combat climate change. And there is certainly symbolic value to the United States rolling back its oil industry tax breaks, possibly making it easier to persuade other countries to follow suit.

I also want to concede that Erickson very rightly called me out on unclearly discussing the relationship between oil price volatility and the effect on oil prices of removing tax breaks. We definitely know which direction removing subsidies would move prices (up) and global consumption (down). I should have been clearer that my comparison of the frequent swings in oil prices to the tiny price impact of removing subsidies was merely to provide a sense of magnitude, NOT to imply that measurement error washes out our ability to forecast the magnitude of tax reform's price impact, *ceteris paribus*.

Finally, Erickson took issue to my characterization of his paper as "misleading." Indeed, I never meant to imply that he and his co-authors intended to mislead anybody. I still, however, stand by what I meant: that the paper might lead a casual reader to take away an erroneous conclusion by relegating the global oil market model to an appendix and only citing the increase in US emissions in the main body. In my opinion, readers need to know that industry tax breaks have a very small effect on global greenhouse gas emissions, but there are other very important reasons to remove them. And yes, the United States absolutely should remove its tax breaks, as should other countries remove their fossil fuel subsidies. On that count, Erickson and I are in complete agreement.

Large-Scale Energy Storage Is a Problem for Renewable Energy

Tom Murphy

Tom Murphy is an associate professor of physics at the University of California, San Diego.

As we look to transition away from fossil fuels, solar and wind are attractive options. Key factors making them compelling are: the inexhaustibility of the source with use (i.e., renewable); their low carbon footprint; and the independence that small-scale distribution can foster (I'll never put a nuclear plant on my roof, even if it would make me the coolest physicist ever!).

But solar and wind suffer a serious problem in that they are not always available. There are windless days, there are sunless nights, and worst of all, there are windless nights. Obviously, this calls for energy storage, allowing us to collect the energy when we *can*, and use it when we *want*.

Small-scale off-grid solar and wind installations have been doing this for a long time, typically using lead-acid batteries as the storage medium. I myself have four golf-cart batteries in my garage storing the energy from eight 130 W solar panels, and use these to power the majority of my electricity consumption at home.

It's worth pausing to appreciate this fact. Compare this scheme to the dream source of fusion. Why do people go ga-ga over fusion? Because there is enough deuterium in water (sea water is fine) to provide a seemingly inexhaustible source of energy, and there are no atmospheric emissions in the process. Meanwhile, solar provides a source that will last longer (billions of years), produces even *less* pollution (no radioactive contamination of containment vessel), and is here today! It's even affordable enough and low-tech enough to be *on my roof and in my garage*! People—we have arrived!

"A Nation-Sized Battery," by Tom Murphy, The Oil Drum, August 10, 2011. http://www.theoildrum.com/pdf/theoildrum_8237.pdf. Licensed under CC BY-SA 3.0 US

Storage works on the small scale, as many stand-aloners can attest. How would it scale up? Can it?

Meeting Requirements

So what would it take? We're not a nation tolerant of power outages. Those big refrigerators can spoil a lot of food when the electricity drops away. A rule of thumb for remote solar installations is that you should design your storage to last for a minimum of three days with no energy input. Even then, sometimes you will "go dark" in the worst storm of the winter. This does not mean literally three days of total deprivation, but could be four consecutive days at 25% average input, so that you only haul in one day's worth over a four day period, leaving yourself short by three.

So let's buy ourselves security and design a battery that can last a week without any new inputs (as before, this is not literally 7 days of zero input, but could be 8 days at 12.5% average input or 10 days at 30% input). This may be able to manage the worst-case "perfect" storm of persistent clouds in the desert Southwest plus weak wind in the Plains.

Let's also plan ahead and have *all* of our country's energy needs met by this system: transportation, heating, industry, etc. The rate at which we currently use energy in all forms in the US is 3 TW. If we transition everything to electricity, we can get by with 2 TW, assuming no growth in demand. Why? Because we currently use two-thirds of our energy supply (or 2 TW) to run heat engines, getting only about 0.6 TW out for useful purposes in the bargain. An electrical system could deliver this same 0.6 TW for only 1 TW of input, considering storage and transmission efficiencies.

Running a 2 TW electrified country for 7 days requires 336 billion kWh of storage. We could also use nuclear power as a baseload to offset a significant portion of the need for storage— perhaps chopping the need in two. This post deals with the narrower topic of what it would take to implement a full-scale renewable-energy battery. Scale the result as you see fit.

The National Battery

Putting the pieces together, our national battery occupies a volume of 4.4 billion cubic meters, equivalent to a cube 1.6 km (one mile) on a side. The size in itself is not a problem: we'd naturally break up the battery and distribute it around the country. This battery would demand 5 trillion kg (5 billion tons) of lead.

Get the Lead Out!

A USGS report from 2011 reports 80 million tons (Mt) of lead in known reserves worldwide, with 7 Mt in the US. A note in the report indicates that the recent demonstration of lead associated with zinc, silver, and copper deposits places the estimated (undiscovered) lead resources of the world at 1.5 billion tons. That's still not enough to build the battery for the US alone. We could chose to be optimistic and assume that more lead will be identified over time. But let's not ignore completely the fact that at this moment in time, no one can point to a map of the world and tell you where even 2% of the necessary lead would come from to build a lead-acid battery big enough for the US. And even the undiscovered but suspected lead falls short.

What about cost? At today's price for lead, $2.50/kg, the national battery would cost $13 trillion in lead alone, and perhaps double this to fashion the raw materials into a battery (today's deep cycle batteries retail for four times the cost of the lead within them). But I guarantee that if we really want to use more lead than we presently estimate to exist in deposits, we're *not* dealing with *today's* prices. Leaving this caveat aside, the naïve $25 trillion price tag is more than the annual US GDP. Recall that lead-acid is currently the *cheapest* battery technology. Even if we sacrificed 5% of our GDP to build this battery (would be viewed as a *huge* sacrifice; nearly a trillion bucks a year), the project would take decades to complete.

But even then, we aren't done: batteries are good for only so many cycles (roughly 1000, depending on depth of discharge), so the national battery would require a rotating service schedule to recycle each part once every 5 years or so. This servicing would be a massive, expensive, and never-ending undertaking.

Who Needs Lead-Acid?

I focus here on lead-acid because it's the devil we know; it's the cheapest storage at present, and the materials are far more abundant than lithium (13 Mt reserves worldwide, 33 Mt estimated global resources), or nickel (76 Mt global reserves, 130 Mt estimated land resources worldwide). If we ever got serious about building big storage, there will be choices other than lead-acid. But I nonetheless find it immensely instructive (and daunting) to understand what it *would* mean to scale a mature technology to meet our needs. It worries me that the cheapest solution we have today would break the bank just based on today's cost of raw materials, and that we can't even identify enough in the world to get the job done.

This post does not proclaim that there is no way to build adequate storage to accommodate a fully-renewable energy infrastructure. A distributed grid helps, and an armada of gas-fired peak-load plants would offset the need for full storage. Storage can be augmented by pumped hydro, compressed air, flywheels, other battery technologies, etc.

Rather, the lesson is that we must work within serious constraints to meet future demands. We can't just scale up the current go-to solution for renewable energy storage—we are yet again fresh out of silver bullet solutions. More generally, large-scale energy storage is *not* a solved problem. We should be careful not to trivialize the problem, which tends to reduce the imperative to work like mad on establishing adequate capabilities in time (requires decades of fore-thought and planning).

Environmental Impacts from Wind Energy

Union of Concerned Scientists

The Union of Concerned Scientists puts rigorous, independent science to work to solve our planet's most pressing problems.

H arnessing power from the wind is one of the cleanest and most sustainable ways to generate electricity as it produces no toxic pollution or global warming emissions. Wind is also abundant, inexhaustible, and affordable, which makes it a viable and large-scale alternative to fossil fuels.

Despite its vast potential, there are a variety of environmental impacts associated with wind power generation that should be recognized and mitigated.

Land Use

The land use impact of wind power facilities varies substantially depending on the site: wind turbines placed in flat areas typically use more land than those located in hilly areas. However, wind turbines do not occupy all of this land; they must be spaced approximately 5 to 10 rotor diameters apart (a rotor diameter is the diameter of the wind turbine blades). Thus, the turbines themselves and the surrounding infrastructure (including roads and transmission lines) occupy a small portion of the total area of a wind facility.

A survey by the National Renewable Energy Laboratory of large wind facilities in the United States found that they use between 30 and 141 acres per megawatt of power output capacity (a typical new utility-scale wind turbine is about 2 megawatts). However, less than 1 acre per megawatt is disturbed permanently and less than 3.5 acres per megawatt are disturbed temporarily during

"Environmental Impacts of Wind Power," Union of Concerned Scientists, http://www.ucsusa.org/clean-energy/renewable-energy/environmental-impacts-wind-power#.WhJtM-dx0dU. Reprinted by permission.

construction. The remainder of the land can be used for a variety of other productive purposes, including livestock grazing, agriculture, highways, and hiking trails. Alternatively, wind facilities can be sited on brownfields (abandoned or underused industrial land) or other commercial and industrial locations, which significantly reduces concerns about land use.

Offshore wind facilities, which are currently not in operation in the United States but may become more common, require larger amounts of space because the turbines and blades are bigger than their land-based counterparts. Depending on their location, such offshore installations may compete with a variety of other ocean activities, such as fishing, recreational activities, sand and gravel extraction, oil and gas extraction, navigation, and aquaculture. Employing best practices in planning and siting can help minimize potential land use impacts of offshore and land-based wind projects.

Wildlife and Habitat

The impact of wind turbines on wildlife, most notably on birds and bats, has been widely document and studied. A recent National Wind Coordinating Committee (NWCC) review of peer-reviewed research found evidence of bird and bat deaths from collisions with wind turbines and due to changes in air pressure caused by the spinning turbines, as well as from habitat disruption. The NWCC concluded that these impacts are relatively low and do not pose a threat to species populations.

Additionally, research into wildlife behavior and advances in wind turbine technology have helped to reduce bird and bat deaths. For example, wildlife biologists have found that bats are most active when wind speeds are low. Using this information, the Bats and Wind Energy Cooperative concluded that keeping wind turbines motionless during times of low wind speeds could reduce bat deaths by more than half without significantly affecting power production. Other wildlife impacts can be mitigated through better siting of wind turbines. The US Fish and Wildlife Services has played a leadership role in this effort by convening an advisory group including representatives from industry, state and tribal governments, and nonprofit organizations that made comprehensive recommendations on appropriate wind farm siting and best management practices.

Offshore wind turbines can have similar impacts on marine birds, but as with onshore wind turbines, the bird deaths associated with offshore wind are minimal. Wind farms located offshore will also impact fish and other marine wildlife. Some studies suggest that turbines may actually increase fish populations by acting as artificial reefs. The impact will vary from site to site, and therefore proper research and monitoring systems are needed for each offshore wind facility.

Public Health and Community

Sound and visual impact are the two main public health and community concerns associated with operating wind turbines. Most of the sound generated by wind turbines is aerodynamic, caused by the movement of turbine blades through the air. There is also mechanical sound generated by the turbine itself. Overall sound levels depend on turbine design and wind speed.

Some people living close to wind facilities have complained about sound and vibration issues, but industry and government-sponsored studies in Canada and Australia have found that these issues do not adversely impact public health. However, it is important for wind turbine developers to take these community concerns seriously by following "good neighbor" best practices for siting turbines and initiating open dialogue with affected community members. Additionally, technological advances, such as minimizing blade surface imperfections and using sound-absorbent materials can reduce wind turbine noise.

Under certain lighting conditions, wind turbines can create an effect known as shadow flicker. This annoyance can be minimized with careful siting, planting trees or installing window awnings, or curtailing wind turbine operations when certain lighting conditions exist.

The Federal Aviation Administration (FAA) requires that large wind turbines, like all structures over 200 feet high, have white or red lights for aviation safety. However, the FAA recently determined that as long as there are no gaps in lighting greater than a half-mile, it is not necessary to light each tower in a multi-turbine wind project. Daytime lighting is unnecessary as long as the turbines are painted white.

When it comes to aesthetics, wind turbines can elicit strong reactions. To some people, they are graceful sculptures; to others, they are eyesores that compromise the natural landscape. Whether a community is willing to accept an altered skyline in return for cleaner power should be decided in an open public dialogue.

Water Use

There is no water impact associated with the operation of wind turbines. As in all manufacturing processes, some water is used to manufacture steel and cement for wind turbines.

Life-Cycle Global Warming Emissions

While there are no global warming emissions associated with operating wind turbines, there are emissions associated with other stages of a wind turbine's life-cycle, including materials production, materials transportation, on-site construction and assembly, operation and maintenance, and decommissioning and dismantlement.

Estimates of total global warming emissions depend on a number of factors, including wind speed, percent of time the wind is blowing, and the material composition of the wind turbine. Most estimates of wind turbine life-cycle global warming emissions are between 0.02 and 0.04 pounds of carbon dioxide equivalent per kilowatt-hour. To put this into context, estimates of life-cycle global warming emissions for natural gas generated electricity are between 0.6 and 2 pounds of carbon dioxide equivalent per kilowatt-hour and estimates for coal-generated electricity are 1.4 and 3.6 pounds of carbon dioxide equivalent per kilowatt-hour.

The Footprint of Renewables Is Larger than Expected

Hans Verolme

Hans Verolme is founder and senior strategic adviser at Climate Advisers Network.

Water and wind power have been in widespread use for centuries. Since the 1880s hydro-power from dams has been harnessed for electricity generation and has provided a significant share of electricity production worldwide. Until the Second World War, windmills were widespread in rural areas for pumping water, but they were rarely used for power generation. Only since the 1973 oil crisis have wind and solar energy gained ground. These renewable technologies struggled to grow their market share due to relatively low efficiency and high upfront investment costs. Over the past decade, we have witnessed a revolutionary transition with the price of wind energy and solar photo-voltaics now at or near grid parity.[1] Four decades of public investment in R&D have fueled innovation with a focus on improved efficiency. Public support for small-scale and community-owned generation through e.g. feed-in tariffs have contributed to this silent revolution.

Traditional critiques of renewables have focused on the intermittency of wind and solar power and their high upfront investment costs. As the use of renewable technology became more widespread, research and development turned to addressing intermittency through new energy storage and smart grid solutions. In Germany today, with 25% of electricity generated by grid-connected renewables, grid stability is not a problem.

Today, we are most critical of the further development of large hydro-power dam projects and the development of biofuels as an alternative to fossil fuels.

Hydro-Power

Historically, hydro-power generated by large dams has become associated with negative social and environmental impacts. A dam interrupts and can permanently decrease the flow of the river, which often harms the ecosystem. Lack of consultation of affected communities has been the norm. Flooding a basin often leads to loss of fertile land. Forced relocations have led to human rights abuses. Many of the affected communities have literally seen development pass them by. This led to a strong and growing anti-dam movement. In response to the loss of public support for hydro-development, the independent World Commission on Dams in 1998 prepared stringent recommendations for any further hydro-power development. Unfortunately, the sensible recommendations of the WCD have been treated as optional by governments and business. We observe a trend towards more investment in small and in-stream hydro-power projects with a small footprint. Opposition to mega-projects remains strong and investments have decreased.

Increasingly, old large hydro-power dams are being redeveloped after several decades of use. The dams have often seen capacity drop significantly due to siltation of the basin. The redeveloped dams can be fitted with the latest generation efficient turbines. At the same time, large dams are sensitive to climate change. The flow of rivers is disproportionally affected by a drop in precipitation. As a result, power generation becomes less reliable and redevelopment uneconomical.

Biofuels and Biomass

Many conventional coal-fired power plants use biomass or municipal waste to co-fire their plants. Similarly, many waste incinerators need biomass to operate and generate heat and power. Co-firing of biomass from often poorly managed forests to make the energy mix more 'green' is plain wrong. The use of municipal waste can also deprive communities of waste pickers of their livelihood, or biomass from supposedly 'marginal lands' deprives herders from traditional sources of fodder. Furthermore, incineration is a major source of toxic air pollution.

Biomass and biofuels have incorrectly been characterized as carbon-neutral. Cultivating, harvesting and transporting biomass also generates a considerable amount of emissions. Processing or incineration of biomass and biofuels often produces dangerous gasses, such as NO_x, carbon monoxide and soot.

Biofuels are expected to gradually replace fuels from oil. The first generation of biofuels are made from sugar, starch or vegetable oil, all agricultural products that compete for valuable arable land with food crops. They also need clean water and other inputs, such as fertilizers and pesticides, to grow. These agricultural inputs require significant energy and resources in their production.

Wind Energy

Wind energy does not leave behind a scarred landscape, like a coal mine. Yet, its growing impact on the landscape and wildlife has been closely scrutinized by conservationists. Like other large scale development projects, wind and concentrated solar projects require environmental impact assessment. The siting decisions need to take into account migration routes of raptors, potential noise impacts on bats and, in the case of offshore parks, the potential impact on marine and migrating birdlife. Interestingly, as wind mills have grown in size and capacity (the largest mills a rated between 3 and 5 MW with 50% net capacity) designers were forced to change the blade design to make them lighter and less noisy. In Europe many farmers happily agree to leasing a corner of their fields to a windmill, bringing an additional revenue stream with little risk on their part.

Some privileged communities oppose wind parks in scenic landscapes, arguing they are ugly or devalue their land. This is called NIMBYism (from: Not In My Back Yard). Fact is that land ownership and access and usufruct rights need to be respected in project development, something many development initiatives have ignored in the past. Beauty is in the eye of the beholder. For someone growing up around windmills this criticism sounds far fetched.

Non-Renewable Resources for Renewables

Finally, we sometimes forget that even clean technology may require resources that are not, yet, sustainably produced. The manufacturing of solar panels, for example, requires rare, often times toxic, metals which cannot be acquired from sustainable sources. Wind turbines are made using copper and rare earth metals. These can however be recycled once the turbines have come to the end of their productive life. Designers now use cradle-to-cradle design processes to reduce the footprint of products, reuse materials and mimic biological processes in an effort to prevent waste. There is a long way to go.

From this brief overview it becomes evident that our consumption of energy, even with clean renewable technologies is not without consequence. It is important to understand that long-term sustainability can only be achieved by avoiding energy use. Avoiding comes before reducing one's footprint by using only the cleanest and most efficient technologies. This may sound odd in a world where billions lack access to even the most basic energy needs. Indeed, this is not an argument against the concerted campaign to bring clean power to all. The potential for long-term sustainability lies with the rich, regardless where they live, who take much more than their fair share. It is over-consumption of dirty energy that is the problem.

CHAPTER 2

Should We Continue to Use Coal As an Energy Source?

The Coal Industry Provides Jobs to Millions, But Its Future Is Uncertain

Benjamin von Brackel

Benjamin von Brackel is a freelance journalist who specializes in climate and social policy.

In 2012, an estimated seven million people were employed in the coal industry, most of them in coal and lignite mining. That number is likely to be lower in 2015, with employment falling especially in China. The world's largest coal producer is beginning to exploit its reserves more efficiently, however, it still needs many more workers than the United States, where modern equipment and optimized operations enable about 90,000 people to mine 0.9 billion tonnes, mainly in open-cast mines. In China, 5.7 million people are needed to dig out 3.7 billion tonnes, mainly from underground mines. In the United States 10,000 jobs were lost in 2013 alone, partly because the shale-gas boom has made coal production less profitable.

Fewer workers are needed in countries where productivity is rising quickly. For example, the Chinese government has closed thousands of small, inefficient mines. India also needs fewer workers to produce the same amount of coal. Coal India, the state-controlled producer, slimmed its employee rolls from 500,000 in 2005 to 350,000 in 2014. In the same period, its output rose by one-third. Moreover, both India and China have invested in Australian mines to boost their own supplies. These extensive coal imports mean that Australia is one of the few countries where employment in the coal sector was rising in the last decade.

The European Union is also cutting thousands of jobs every year. In 2008, 342,000 miners worked above and below ground; in

2013 the number was only 326,000. In the Czech Republic, which relies heavily on coal, there has been a decrease in employment in the coal sector. After a delay, structural change is now starting in Poland, which obtains most of its energy from coal. Britain has almost completed the transition: by 2016 only two pits will still be in operation, an old mine and a new one, both owned by their workforces.

In 1950, almost 540,000 people worked in Germany's hard coal mines, and 360,000 of them underground. Today the figure is 12,100, and by 2018 there will be no miners underground. In the country's lignite mines, the number of people directly employed in digging out the rock and transforming it into electricity has fallen from 130,000 in 1990 to 21,000 today.

While coal is declining as a source of employment around the world, renewables are growing in importance. In 2013, 6.5 million people were employed in this sector, 800,000 more than in the previous year, according to the International Renewable Energy Agency. This organization estimates that the coal and renewables sectors now employ a similar number of people worldwide. In Germany and the rest of the European Union, jobs in renewables have overtaken those in coal. In developing countries and emerging markets, however, employment figures cover only the coal industry itself, and do not include the related project development, transport and power-plant operations.

Despite such uncertainties, it is still possible to discern some trends. China is the leading power in renewable energy, employing 2.6 million people in 2013. Most jobs can be found in the production and installation of renewable-energy plants. Brazil follows with around 900,000 jobs, the USA with 600,000 and India with 400,000. Germany is fifth. Its employment in renewables has doubled since 2004; by 2013 it had reached 370,000. By comparison, the German lignite industry directly and indirectly employs 70,000 people.

Working conditions in the renewables sector are generally better than in coal, although the renewables still entails risks, as in the chemicals companies that make solar cells. But workers in coal mines are subject to much greater risk to life and limb. And to their lungs, where the coal dust settles causing chronic diseases. Mining accidents are often dramatic, claim many lives, and attract a lot of publicity. With 150 years of experience underground, the coal industry has a deep understanding of the risks, and has detailed regulations to prevent accidents. If accidents occur, they are usually due to safety precautions that have been ignored in order to save costs, to negligence, or to equipment failure.

The situation in China, which accounted for 80 percent of worldwide deaths in coal mining, is improving. The small mines that are being closed are also the most dangerous. In the 1990s, 5,000 to 7,000 miners died every year. In 2010 the figure was 2,400, and 930 in 2014, according to governmental data.

In the western world, the image of a miner is still one of a hard-working, soot-covered man. And indeed, in Europe or Canada—and also in India—women still account for less than 20 percent of the workforce. In the ex-socialist countries, however, more women go underground. In many parts of the world it is not easy for women to find work in the coal industry. And if they do land a job, they are usually paid less than men and have to fear sexual assault in the mine.

According to a Greenpeace study, the coal industry will shed another two to three million jobs by 2030. The renewables sector is growing fast enough to compensate for these losses. In 2014, the Ibbenbüren mine in Germany recruited 56 maintenance trainees. It was the last such hiring.

Coal Carbon Capture, Use, and Storage May Be the Golden Ticket

The World Coal Association

The World Coal Association is the global network for the coal industry. Formed from major international coal producers, it works to demonstrate and gain acceptance for the fundamental role coal plays in achieving a sustainable, lower carbon energy future.

Carbon capture, use and storage (CCUS) is an integrated suite of technologies that can capture up to 90% of the CO_2 emissions produced from the use of fossil fuels in electricity generation and industrial processes, preventing the CO_2 from entering the atmosphere.

Capture

Capture technologies allow the separation of CO_2 from gases produced in electricity generation and industrial processes by one of three methods:

- Pre-combustion capture
- Post-combustion capture
- Oxyfuel combustion

Transportation

CO_2 is then transported for safe use or storage. Millions of tonnes of CO_2 are already transported annually for commercial purposes by pipelines, ships and road tanker. The US has four decades of experience of transporting CO_2 by pipeline for enhanced oil recovery projects.

"Carbon capture, use & storage," World Coal Association. Reprinted by permission.

Use and Storage

Use

CO_2 can be used as a value-added commodity. This can result in a portion of the CO_2 being permanently stored—for example, in concrete that has been cured using CO_2 or in plastic materials derived from biomass that uses CO_2 as one of the ingredients. The CO_2 can also be converted into biomass. This can be achieved, for example, through algae farming using CO_2 as a feedstock. The harvested algae can then be processed into bio-fuels that take the place of non-biological carbon sources.

Enhanced Oil Recovery

CO_2 is already widely used in the oil industry for enhanced oil recovery (EOR) from mature oilfields. When CO_2 is injected into an oilfield it can mix with the crude oil causing it to swell and thereby reducing its viscosity, helping to maintain or increase the pressure in the reservoir. The combination of these processes allows more of the crude oil to flow to the production wells. In other situations, the CO_2 is not soluble in the oil. Here, injection of CO_2 raises the pressure in the reservoir, helping to sweep the oil towards the production well. In EOR, the CO_2 can therefore have a positive commercial value and can help support the deployment of CCUS and create a revenue stream for CCS projects, as the CO_2 captured becomes an economic resource.

Storage

CO_2 is stored in carefully selected geological rock formations that are typically located several kilometres below the earth's surface. As CO_2 is pumped deep underground, it is compressed by the higher pressures and becomes essentially a liquid. There are a number of different types of geological trapping mechanisms (depending on the physical and chemical characteristics of the rocks and fluids) that can be utilised for CO_2 storage.

At every point in the CCUS chain, from production to storage, industry has at its disposal a number of process technologies that are well understood and have excellent health and safety records. The commercial deployment of CCUS will involve the widespread adoption of these CCUS techniques, combined with robust monitoring techniques and government regulation.

CCUS Costs

All the options for capturing CO_2 from power generation have higher capital and operating costs as well as lower efficiencies than conventional power plants without capture. Capture is typically the most expensive part of the CCS chain. However, as CCS and power generation technology become more efficient and better integrated, the increased energy use is likely to fall significantly below early levels. Much of the work on capture is focused on lowering costs and improving efficiency as well as improving the integration of the capture and power generation components. These improvements will reduce energy requirements.

EOR can also help support the deployment of CCUS and create a revenue stream for CCS projects as the CO_2 captured becomes an economic resource.

CCUS Today

There are currently 22 large-scale integrated CCS projects in operation or under construction. Significant projects include:

Boundary Dam Power Station
The world's first large-scale CCS project in the power sector commenced operation in October 2014 at the Boundary Dam power station in Saskatchewan, Canada.

Petra Nova
Petra Nova, which came online in early 2017 and is the second CCUS coal plant, is the world's largest post-combustion carbon capture facility installed on an existing coal-fuelled power plant and plans to store more than 1.6 million tonnes of CO_2 a year.

The Sleipner and Snøhvit CO_2 Storage Projects
These projects in Norway have stored over 16 million tonnes of CO_2 into offshore deep saline formations.

Great Plains Synfuels Weyburn-Midale

Since 2000, about 3 million tonnes of CO_2 a year has been captured from a synthetic natural gas plant at Great Plains in the US, and transported for EOR operations at the Weyburn-Midale oilfields, in Canada.

Role of CCUS in Global Climate Action

CCUS is an important option in global efforts to reduce CO_2 emissions. Research from the Intergovernmental Panel on Climate Change (IPCC) has shown that climate action will be 140% more expensive without carbon capture and storage and that meeting the 2°C target could actually be impossible without it.

Boundary Dam CCUS Project

The Boundary Dam Project sees the integration of a rebuilt coal-fired generation unit with carbon capture technology, resulting in low-emission power generation. Launched in 2014, the project is the world's first post-combustion coal-fired CCS project.

The project transforms the aging Unit #3 at Boundary Dam Power Station near Estevan, Saskatchewan into a reliable, long-term producer of 110 megawatts (MW) of base-load electricity and reduces greenhouse gas emissions by one million tonnes of CO_2 each year. That's equivalent to taking more than 250,000 cars off Saskatchewan roads annually.

The captured CO_2 is transported by pipeline to nearby oil fields in southern Saskatchewan where it is used for enhanced oil recovery. CO_2 not used for enhanced oil recovery is stored in the Aquistore Project.

In addition to CO_2, there are opportunities for the sale of other byproducts from the project. Sulphur dioxide (SO_2) will be captured, converted to sulphuric acid and sold for industrial use. Fly ash, a by-product of coal combustion, will also be sold for use in ready-mix concrete, pre-cast structures and concrete products.

The US Hit the Jackpot with Coal

Fred Beach

Fred Beach is a fellow at the Center for International Energy and Environmental Policy (Jackson School of Geosciences), the Webber Energy Group (Department of Mechanical Engineering), and the McCombs Business School at the University of Texas at Austin.

I n recent years, every time an election has rolled around, politicians have espoused the necessity of energy independence and energy security. According to them, if we are to achieve the necessary level of energy security we need to "drill, baby, drill," develop "clean coal," install new pipelines, develop renewable energy, make sure our cars get better gas mileage, or [fill in another sound bite of your choosing here]. A listener could easily conclude that the US lacks energy security. But what do the numbers tell us about our current state of independence? And is the political sloganeering grounded in fact, or does it ignore how much our situation has changed already?

A History of American Independence

From the time the United States was founded through the last years of World War II, the country was nearly 100 percent energy independent. Electricity came from coal- and oil-fired power plants and a series of massive hydroelectric dams. We had historically produced more petroleum than we used, resulting in our being a net petroleum exporter. However, the explosive growth of our economy following the war and the associated demand for energy (particularly in transportation) outstripped our growth in energy production.

By the second half of the 20th century, our growing demand for electricity resulted in a nationwide electric grid served by central

"Why is the US so insecure about its energy security? Measures of energy independence show it is increasing, not decreasing," by Fred Beach, © 2013 American Geosciences Institute, April 28, 2013. Reprinted by permission.

power plants fueled not just by domestic coal and hydropower, but also by a growing portion of nuclear energy and natural gas. Petroleum had become too expensive to be burned for producing electricity and was used principally for transportation. We were still able to meet most electric power needs domestically, but by 1972, when US petroleum and petroleum liquids production peaked and began a steady, and many thought permanent, decline, we were beginning to import more and more petroleum to fuel our swelling transportation sector.

By 1998, the US was importing half of its petroleum. In 2005, US petroleum imports reached 60 percent of our national consumption and 18 percent of natural gas. Both were all-time highs and combined to result in another record that year as well: Fully 31 percent of total energy consumed in the US came from imported sources.

Just six years later, however, petroleum imports dropped back down to 46 percent, natural gas was down to 6 percent and US dependence on imports for total energy consumption was down to 19 percent.

The trend in increasing energy dependence had not only stopped but had reversed direction in less than a decade. Furthermore, forecasts by the US Energy Information Administration (EIA) predict that by 2035, petroleum liquids imports will have declined further, to 36 percent of consumption; the US will be a net exporter of natural gas; and imports for total energy consumption will be down to 13 percent.

What happened? What does it mean for the US economy and for international relations? Or does it really make any difference at all?

The "Big Three"

The world's current supply of energy is dominated by the "Big Three": petroleum, coal and natural gas. We may aspire to a clean energy future, but for the time being, 87 percent of the world's energy and 82 percent of our nation's energy comes from these three fossil fuels. Consequently, domestic resources of fossil fuels heavily influence the degree to which a nation can achieve energy independence.

There are exceptions to the Big Three dependence. Norway, with a small population and large hydropower resources, obtains 98 percent of its electricity from hydropower. The country's North Sea oil and gas resources fulfill their remaining energy needs while also positioning Norway as the world's second-largest natural gas exporter and Europe's largest oil exporter. But Norway isn't just an exception; it is an anomaly. Then again, so is the US.

The US is the world's third-largest petroleum producer, second-largest coal producer and largest natural gas producer. (We are also number one in nuclear energy generation and number two in wind power generation.) Unfortunately, we are also the world's largest petroleum and natural gas consumer and second-largest coal consumer. It seems that our achievements in energy production are only exceeded by our achievements in energy consumption.

Petroleum

If the US has an Achilles heel in terms of energy security and energy independence, it is petroleum. While the US is the third-largest producer worldwide, our demand far outstrips our production. In fact, until recently, US demand even exceeded the production capacity of the two largest global producers—Saudi Arabia and Russia—combined. But that has changed. Our demand dipped starting in 2005, and the drop-off then accelerated further due to the economic downturn. In addition, during this same period, our production began to increase. By 2011, the US was still the third-largest producer, but domestic production had posted its fourth year of steady growth after nearly three decades of decline.

The bulk of the increase has come from accessing "tight oil" in formations that were previously deemed cost-prohibitive for production when oil sold in the $20 to $40 per barrel price range from the 1980s to early 2000s. The surge of oil prices above $40 per barrel starting in 2004 led oil producers to begin working to access these tight oil deposits. New supply began reaching the market in 2008 and has been increasing every year since. Much of this work in tight oil has occurred in the Bakken shale formation of North Dakota and Montana. But there are several similar formations in the US, such as the Eagle Ford shale in southern Texas, that are in early stages of development.

By 2015, if current production trends continue, the US could surpass both Saudi Arabia and Russia to become the world's largest producer of petroleum liquids. Of course, we won't become a net exporter, but as our production grows faster than our demand, the amount and percentage that we import will steadily decrease.

That decrease won't be evenly distributed across all import sources: Consumption of petroleum from Canada, our largest foreign source, should rise over time. Canada plans to continue developing its oil resources, and new pipeline infrastructure is being built that will essentially "lock in" much of that supply to the US. Our second-largest foreign source of petroleum is Mexico, which has large reserves, in spite of recent decreases in production.

Thus, the decrease in imports will likely occur in the most distant sources (which have the highest transportation costs) such as Saudi Arabia, Iraq and Nigeria. The net effect would be that Canada, which supplied 23 percent of US petroleum imports in 2011, might provide 43 percent by 2035. Over the same period, oil from the Persian Gulf could drop from 16 percent of our imports today to just 12 percent, meaning it would account for an almost negligible 4 percent of our overall consumption.

Of course, production and consumption projections for petroleum are challenging and represent best guesses. Forecasting production is perhaps easier, as it is based on exploration that has already been conducted and on infrastructure projects that have already commenced, even though they may take several years to bear fruit.

Consumption projections are heavily dependent on consumer behavior, such as how much we drive, which is difficult to predict.

Private vehicles account for 62 percent of our petroleum demand and transportation as a whole for more than 70 percent. When gasoline prices increase significantly, people tend to drive less, so consumption goes down. In addition, when prices increase significantly and stay high, politicians and the public call for more efficient vehicles. For projections from now through 2035, EIA's data rely on an average consumer's annual amount of driving and a 40 percent increase in the fuel efficiency of light-duty vehicles. Of course, a stronger consumer movement toward more fuel-efficient vehicles could cause the slow forecast growth in consumption to flatten or even decrease. Additionally, a more rapid adoption of electric and/or natural gas vehicles could also reduce consumption and further reduce petroleum imports.

Coal

It has often been said that the US is the Saudi Arabia of coal. With the world's largest coal reserves, the US has more than 240 years of supply based on current production. What is new is that even though US coal consumption has been in a slow decline since 2007, production has remained roughly constant. That is because our net coal exports have doubled since 2005. For decades, the US has exported metallurgical coal, used in steel production. The recent growth has been in the export of thermal coal for electricity production, the very segment of consumption that is in decline in the US.

Europe has traditionally been the primary customer for US thermal coal. But in 2009, the increased demand for US coal in Europe was matched by demand growth in China. China is the world's top coal producer, but also the top consumer. In 2010 and 2011, China consumed as much coal as the rest of the world combined. And these years were no anomaly. Despite the global economic downturn, China's coal consumption has been growing at an average annual rate of 10 percent since 2001. China has large reserves of coal, but their consumption is so great that they could be exhausted in a little more than 30 years.

Aging coal-fired power plants in the eastern and central US have already begun to be retired, and the pace of this scale back is predicted to increase. Their electric power output will be replaced by a combination of natural gas-fired power plants, wind generation and possibly nuclear plants. The Appalachian coal production that fueled these retiring plants will continue to shift toward export, via Atlantic and Gulf of Mexico ports, to meet the growing demand in Europe and South America.

Logistics and transportation costs favor meeting the growing Asian coal demand with coal from the Powder River Basin in Wyoming and Montana, the largest deposit of low-sulfur subbituminous coal in the world, which is typically used in power plants. In late February, the US Geological Survey released its first-ever assessment of the entire basin, estimating it holds a total of 1.07 trillion short tons of coal, with 162 billion short tons of it currently being economically recoverable.

Permitting of new and expanded coal export terminals in the Pacific Northwest ports of St. Helens and Coos Bay in Oregon and Bellingham, Longview and others in Washington are in progress— although highly controversial. In spite of the economic benefit of exporting coal from these ports, there is strong environmental opposition for a variety of reasons. It is not clear whether environmental or financial concerns will prevail. However, there is little doubt that the growing demand for coal in China, South Korea, Japan and other Asian countries will continue.

Natural Gas

In the US, the fossil fuel story that has grabbed the most media attention in the last several years is the rapid growth in domestic natural gas production. US natural gas production was roughly steady between 18 trillion and 19 trillion cubic feet (TCF) per year for two decades. The sharp increase in production, beginning in 2008, was driven by exploitation of shale gas formations through the combined technologies of horizontal drilling and hydraulic fracturing. Both technologies have existed for several decades, but their use in tapping narrow horizontal layers of gas-bearing shale was spurred in part by a natural gas price increase that began in 2000.

The lag between the increase in the price of natural gas (in 2000) and the increase in production (in 2008) demonstrates the time required to bring a new resource to market on a large scale. The near-simultaneous rise in natural gas and petroleum production is not a coincidence. Both were driven by price increases that spurred exploration and production in hydrocarbon formations that were cost prohibitive to produce at the prices of the preceding decades. The increase in petroleum production also supports natural gas production, as many oil wells also produce associated gas that can be captured for sale. Likewise, many natural gas wells also produce gas condensates, or "wet gas." These petroleum liquids contribute to the nation's petroleum production numbers and help make these natural gas wells profitable even with low natural gas prices.

If, or when, the US becomes a net exporter of natural gas depends primarily on US demand growth. However, the degree to which the US can export natural gas is heavily dependent on export-capable infrastructure. The US has about a dozen liquefied natural gas terminals built for import. Three of these are in the process of being converted to serve as export terminals, with a combined potential capacity of approximately 2 TCF. The extent to which the export infrastructure expands will be driven by the interaction between domestic and overseas demand.

So What Does It All Mean?

The US is now the world's largest producer of natural gas, and is poised to become the world's largest producer of petroleum within the next five to 10 years. In the grand scheme of energy independence, becoming the largest producer of petroleum and natural gas is probably a good thing, as we will likely continue to be the world's largest consumer of both for at least a few more years. Coincident with this, global coal consumption is growing the fastest of all three fossil fuels, and the US has the world's largest reserves.

Growth in overseas coal demand, coupled with a reduction in domestic demand, seems to indicate that our exports of coal will increase. China's coal production is three times that of the US, so it is unlikely that the US will achieve a fossil fuel production trifecta, but our number two position in coal production will likely continue unchallenged.

All three of these macro-trends in fossil fuel production support a steady reduction in US net energy imports and therefore an increase in US energy independence. Our energy consumption-to-production gap might close over time, meaning imports could account for as little as 13 percent of consumption by 2035, based on EIA projections. The production forecasts might carry a bit more veracity than the consumption figures, but the direction of the trends is likely correct. Growth of US consumption of fossil fuels is slowing and even declining (especially for coal), while the world's as a whole is growing. And while our production of all three is steady or increasing, the world's production is doing all it can to keep up.

However, just what increased energy independence means for the US is unclear. From a security standpoint, reduced reliance on imported petroleum would seem to portend a reduction in our national security interest and involvement in the Middle East and the Persian Gulf states in particular. This probably wouldn't sit well with US allies such as Japan and South Korea, which will still be almost wholly dependent on Middle East oil and on our historical involvement in keeping it flowing to them. Taken to a not unrealistic extreme, the fossil fuel resource wealth of Canada, the US and Mexico could allow the North American continent to create its own energy cartel. This would potentially allow North America to not just set its own price for oil, but to decouple itself entirely from the erratic global energy market and to stabilize oil, gas and coal prices in North America, thereby providing the continent with a huge economic advantage.

From a more pedestrian economic perspective, it would seem to be good to reduce our energy imports and increase our exports.

This would help with our international balance of trade while bolstering domestic employment. With a major trade partner like China, for example, given that we are dependent on them for their products, it might be good to be in a position of having them more dependent upon us to supply the energy resources needed to manufacture those products and grow their economy.

However, history has shown that being more energy independent is not always good for us economically. It was during our time of greatest energy dependence, from 1995 to 2005, that the US economy experienced some of its greatest growth. This might be explained at the macro-level as the result of the relatively low global cost of energy during those years fueling the growth in consumption and productivity in the US. Or put another way, when the global cost of energy was low, we bought more of it from others, and now that it is high, we are making a shift toward buying less abroad and producing more domestically.

The importance of national energy independence for the US is also confusing when the situations of other major countries are considered. For example, of the countries in the G8—the Group of Eight, which have the largest economies in the world (not including China and Brazil)—only Canada and Russia are net energy exporters, that is, 100 percent energy independent. Regardless of how similar in energy independence the two may be, however, they couldn't be more different in how they employ this "advantage" via international relations. Likewise, although both Japan and Italy are more than 80 percent dependent on imports for their energy, the health of their economies and influence in international affairs are very different. Finally, even though Germany already imports more than half of its energy, the country seems comfortable in making energy policy decisions that could make it even more dependent (such as deciding to shutter their nuclear power plants over the next several years).

The future is never clear, but trends in energy production and consumption at the national level do not change quickly. The recent reversal in the US energy balance from four decades of increasing dependence to growth in independence was more than a decade in the making and required concurrent shifts in US production and consumption trends of all three fossil fuels.

But now that the change has occurred, it helps paint the broad strokes of what the next few decades of energy production and consumption might look like. What remains to be seen is whether we will harness this growth in domestic energy development and increase our energy independence to strengthen our economy and bolster our international footing, or if we will squander it away.

Coal Carbon Capture Is a Scam

Greenpeace

Greenpeace is an independent campaigning organization that acts to expose global environmental problems and achieve solutions that are essential to a green and peaceful future.

[...]

Capturing Carbon Will Increase Climate Pollution

Australia, the second largest exporter of coal after Indonesia, announced in 2009 a new initiative called the Global CCS Institute to promote CCS development world-wide. The Institute says the business case for carbon capture rests on the 'twin pillars' of public support and market opportunity. The exorbitant cost of CCS and political difficulty in generating taxpayer support has made proponents turn more and more to market opportunity, at the expense of theoretical integrity in the argument that CCS could help the climate.

CC-EOR Is an Oil Industry Strategy

CCS proponents do not bother to hide that the major selling point behind carbon capture is its role in 'enhanced oil recovery' (EOR)—which is not a better method of cleaning up spilled oil, as one might guess the term means. They aren't recovering oil, since they never had it in the first place. And 'enhanced' doesn't mean any improvement in quality. In fact, the oil is more highly saturated with CO_2, so it's worse for the climate. EOR is a euphemism for increasing oil extraction.

Responsible for 6% of US oil production today, up from virtually nothing in the 1980s, industry claims to have been using CO_2-EOR for more than three decades. CO_2-EOR works by pumping CO_2 underground to force out oil that otherwise could not be extracted. Some claim that without CO_2 injection

65% of the oil would be left underground. In other words, under the auspices of helping the climate, carbon capture will be used to increase oil extraction by as much as 185%.

Currently, CO_2-EOR operations rely mostly on CO_2 extracted directly from natural CO_2 reservoirs, usually in close proximity to oil rigs. Natural CO_2 supplies are exhaustible and really only available in the United States, although the rising demand for anthropogenic CO_2 to increase oil extraction is global. In the Permian Basin demand for CO_2 by the oil industry began to exceed supply in 2004.

The majority of CO_2-EOR operations are in Permian Basin (Texas and New Mexico), where high-quality CO_2 sources reside near oil reservoirs "amenable" to EOR.[7] One analysis called EOR "the main driver behind CCS," which was before federal regulations on GHG emissions. Oil companies, such as BP, view CO_2-EOR as the only way to maintain or increase production. Another analyst rightly noted, "... not only does CCS need CO_2-EOR to help provide economic viability for CCS, but CO_2-EOR also needs CCS in order to ensure adequate carbon dioxide supplies to facilitate growth in production from EOR." In 2010 there were already 129 CO_2-EOR projects—only one was labeled as a CCS project.

The oil industry has viewed carbon capture with EOR (CC-EOR) as a key part of their expansion before any public relations work to greenwash it.

No Green Stamp
The logical foundation of proponents of CC-EOR is presented in a 2012 report commissioned by the National Enhanced Oil Recovery Initiative (NEORI). The report states "[i]n a fortunate, if ironic, twist of fate, a key to increasing America's domestic energy security lies in capturing and productively utilizing a portion of our nation's industrial CO_2 emissions, thereby meeting a critical domestic energy challenge, while also helping to solve a global environmental problem."

NEORI describes itself as a diverse set of constituents. While three of NEORI's 35 members and observers are environmental NGOs, the overwhelming majority have a stake in carbon capture or EOR whether or not there is a climate benefit. They are surely quite happy to call it 'green tech.' NEORI has succeeded in getting their recommendations into legislative proposals, such as tax credits proposed by Senator Jay Rockefeller (D-WV).

Since 95% of oil is extracted to be burned, thus creating more CO_2 pollution, there is no simple logic that using CO_2 to increase oil supply benefits the climate. CC-EOR proponents making a case for the climate therefore must rely on a set of elaborate political economic assumptions.

Even if they admit that there is some reduction in the climate benefit, they must assume that a critical majority of the injected CO_2 eventually stays underground. Unfortunately, this assumption fails. One reason is that extraction companies do not re-capture the CO_2 during production. An analysis of existing CO_2-EOR operations noted that "accounting for CO_2 losses is not typically done for EOR." That is not surprising because for oil companies sequestration of CO_2 is not an objective—growth of their industry is.

There is no reason to believe industry practices are geared toward anything but maximizing oil sales. Creating an incentive for CC-EOR-with-Storage would require heavy carbon taxation, according to the IEA. There is no such policy in the US, and it doesn't appear the Republican-controlled Congress is anywhere near considering a carbon tax.

There are few peer-reviewed studies of lifecycle greenhouse gas emissions from CO_2-EOR projects. However, one study of five projects revealed that—between mining coal capturing carbon from the coal plant, utilizing the carbon for EOR, and burning the produced oil—CC-EOR can result in a net increase in carbon emissions.

Achieving a net reduction in emissions would require making sure that most of the injected CO_2 does not escape with extracted oil, or at least that it is 'recycled' (neither of which the proposed

EPA carbon rule on new coal plants would require). Even then, the practice would have to be industry-wide. If one company were obligated to capture the CO_2 which returns to the surface with extracted oil, the injected CO_2 does not stay confined to one drilling rig's operations. As intended, injected CO_2 becomes mixed and dispersed with the oil underground, which means it can be extracted by other companies' drill rigs as well. Thus, 'recycling' a critical majority of injected CO_2 may not even be physically possible in many cases. There is also the problem of abandoned wells, which the next chapter will discuss.

The second false assumption is that CC-EOR makes strategic sense for scaling up investment in CCS in general. The Global CCS Institute, NEORI, and others claim that this shrewdly harnesses oil industry profit incentive in order to augment overall investment in CCS. This view may be theoretically sound with respect to capital investment in general, and perhaps with achieving economies of scale at some point far into the future (too far to matter for mitigating climate change). But it cannot be true when it comes to building fixed infrastructure. It would not be economical, nor practical, to take a) custom built infrastructure designed to scrub CO_2 from a new lignite-fired power plant in Mississippi to pipe to an oil extraction site less than 100 miles away (i.e., Kemper plant) and then export it to b) retrofit a non-lignite coal plant in China in order to sequester the CO_2.

The NEORI optimism about harnessing private oil investment appears to view oil money as finite and public dollars as limitless— but they have it backwards. Taxpayer dollars are scarce, whereas the 2014 revenue of the top 15 oil companies was about $4 trillion, more than the entire US federal budget. DOE claims to be subsidizing CC-EOR with the aim to encourage CCS at a scale that would benefit the climate, which means it is ignoring its own analysis. A DOE-commissioned study concluded that "[CC-EOR] is unlikely to serve as a major stepping stone to commercial-scale CCS deployment."

The third and most dubious assumption is that oil companies choose not to develop new wells if they can get more out of existing wells. However, one might attempt to make this 'zero sum production' claim more rigorous. Analyst Jaramillo says "[t]he key argument for CO_2-EOR as a sequestration method is that the electricity and oil produced within the system boundary displaces oil or electricity from other sources." For example, assume BP producing oil in the Gulf means Suncor produces less carbon-intensive tar sands oil in Alberta. This economic rationalization made by those with apparent misgivings about supporting CC-EOR is obviously a non sequitur.

Regarding Jaramillo's point about sources of electricity within the system boundary, investing in CC-EOR arguably displaces investments in renewables if it extends the life of a coal plant or results in new coal-fired capacity that wind or solar could otherwise provide.

The aforementioned DOE study found CC-EOR contributes little if anything to CCS deployment in part because CC-EOR momentum exists to make the oil industry more profitable. It is clear that for the industry this is about extracting more oil—growing more as an industry—than they otherwise could. The oil industry's plans for profit growth are not just amoral but myopically oriented toward selling as much oil as possible.

Exxon CEO, Lee Raymond, famously declared that the company was not American and did not make decisions based on what's good for America, but he might as well have said that companies whose aim is making money from oil supply do not make decisions based on what's good for the global economy or even themselves. Climate disruption will impact all of us.

CC-EOR is no more a climate solution than drilling in ultra-deepwater, hydro-fracking, or drilling in the Arctic Ocean. These are just next steps for an industry destroying the climate. Oil companies have turned to EOR to be able to sell more oil, after exhausting more easily obtainable supplies. There is no escaping that, as Jaramillo states, "without displacement of a carbon intensive energy source, CO_2-EOR systems will result in net carbon emissions."

Oil produced from injection of CO_2 captured from coal plants is arguably is worse than conventional oil, since it is part of scheme to either build new coal plants or keep existing plants from shuttering. Emissions from CC-EOR will include emissions from coal extraction, processing, new coal combustion (not all the CO_2 is captured), not to mention combustion of oil that would otherwise stay in the ground.

World-wide, all but three of the thirteen large-scale, carbon-capture projects to have begun operating use the captured CO_2 for EOR operations. None of the three non-EOR operations is a power plant. They are gas extraction operations designed to re-inject underground the CO_2 scrubbed from raw natural gas. One of the three operations, in Algeria, was suspended indefinitely in 2011. The other two are both operated by Statoil in Norway. Statoil avoids paying tens of millions of dollars per year under Norway's carbon tax system.

The Global CCS Institute is of course optimistic that EOR "is promoting early deployment of CCS." However, even if one gives undue acknowledgement to the other 40 carbon capture projects which the Global CCS Institute documents on paper could operate in the next decade, only 9 aim to sequester CO_2 captured from a power plant. FutureGen would have been a 10th and was for quite a while the most likely to succeed. FutureGen was the last remaining large-scale carbon capture power plant project in the US that aimed to sequester its CO_2 pollution.

[...]

CO_2 Capture Will Increase the Environmental Impact of Coal

Let's assume CCS could work as its most idealistic proponents might argue. Assume it isn't being developed for increasing oil extraction, but instead to sequester the CO_2 permanently from the atmosphere. At best, CCS would mitigate some of the carbon pollution associated with burning coal, but it would do nothing to address a long list of many other environmental and public health harms associated with coal use in the power sector. CCS would exacerbate many of these harms not just because it would support continued use of coal, but because power plants using carbon capture require 20% or more coal to provide the same amount of electricity.

Using coal for electricity requires mining, washing and processing, transporting, burning, as well as disposing of ash—in stark contrast with relying on the wind and sun for energy. This last section highlights some of the key ways in which CCS would magnify coal's environmental footprint.

Water Use

Coal-fired power plants are the largest users of freshwater (more than agricultural withdrawal) in the United States, a particular problem for Western and Midwestern states stricken by longer and more extreme droughts caused by climate change. According to the US Department of Energy (DOE), both coal and natural gas-fired power plants with carbon capture would consume far more water, up to twice as much as non-carbon capture plants. Coal plants also release and incredible amount of heated wastewater, damaging local freshwater ecosystems.

Air and Water Pollution

Coal combustion remains a major source of many air pollutants, including sulfur dioxide that causes acid rain and particulate matter that causes health impacts such as asthma.[29] Coal combustion has historically been the number one cause of mercury contamination in US waterways. Half of the navigable lakes and rivers in the United States are closed to fishing and swimming at any given time, the majority because of mercury contamination. New mercury pollution standards will help, but a significant amount of mercury pollution drifts into the United States from coal combustion in other countries such as China. Carbon capture would do nothing to reduce mercury pollution, and could even exacerbate it by producing greater amounts of coal ash.

In addition, drinking water is contaminated by every part of the coal waste stream with chemicals and compounds that cause cancer, birth deformities, and other health issues. This is because the coal industry's contribution to pollution in our rivers, lakes, and seas includes a laundry list of toxic chemicals and compounds, such as cyanide, arsenic, selenium, ammonia, sulfur, sulfate, nitrates, nitric acid, tars, oils, fluorides, chlorides, and other acids and metals, including sodium, iron, thallium, cadmium, beryllium, barium, antimony, and lead.

Toxic Coal Ash

Coal plants using carbon capture will produce more coal ash because the technology requires power to operate—20 to 30% of the coal ash generated per kilowatt hour would be related to carbon capture. After mining waste, coal ash is the largest waste stream in the country, as it is in other countries like China.

Coal ash is laden with other cancer-causing chemicals and heavy metals, and most coal ash produced in recent decades sits in unlined "ponds" that continuously leach into groundwater. Coal ash containment is so negligent that massive quantities have spilled on multiple occasions, contaminating rivers and even wiping out nearby communities. In one infamous case in 2008, 1.1 billion gallons of coal ash slurry (more than oil spilled from the *Exxon Valdez*) spilled from its containment near the TVA Kingston Fossil Plant in Tennessee, forcing evacuations from the town. While new regulations on non-climate air pollutants will lead to cleaner air, it also means coal ash will become more toxic.

In the United States, coal ash has never been regulated federally even though the problem crosses state boundaries, and most states have poor or no regulations on coal ash. The TVA Kingston disaster prompted EPA to consider regulations in 2009, but decided six years later to provide a coal ash guidance in lieu of enforceable standards.

Public Health and the Economy

Coal has a giant, negative impact on the economy. For instance, coal transport has traditionally dominated US rail capacity. In the United States, transporting coal has been responsible for a quarter of the carloads and half of the tonnage carried by train, although this has fallen in recent years with declining coal demand. Coal trains can spill toxic dust along their path, can catch fire spontaneously, and generally get in the way of using railways for public transportation and transporting other commodities. Industry plans to build new export terminals in the Pacific Northwest, threatening to increase its already massive footprint on transportation infrastructure.

Adding up the monetized life cycle costs of coal used for electricity, such as health costs from its pollution and environmental cleanup, comes to as much as $523 billion per year in the United States on top of the price of electricity—$308 billion if climate-related costs are excluded. A 2010 Harvard study assessed the costs of coal pollution that result from lost work hours and lowered productivity due to various health conditions, including mental retardation (from mercury), cancer, cardiovascular disease, black lung and other pulmonary diseases, transport fatalities, asthma, and early death. While the study admitted the true ecological and health costs are worse, it concluded that "[a]ccounting for the many external costs over the life cycle for coal-derived electricity conservatively doubles to triples the price of coal per kWh of electricity generated."

[…]

Behind the Scenes of Coal

Douglas Fischer

Douglas Fischer is editor of The Daily Climate, *an independent news site covering energy, the environment, and climate change.*

L arry Gibson lives on an island in the sky.

It didn't start that way: His land was once a low hill in a rugged hardwood forest—cherry, oak, hickory—skipping from ridge to ridge across one of the poorest, most rural areas of the Lower 48.

Then came the mining companies with their dynamite and trucks. They clear-cut the forest, blew the tops off the ridges and scraped the rocks into the hollows, pushing hundreds of feet of mountains into the valleys below.

They came for the coal—energy that provides half of the nation's electricity and has been touted as a major plank in the United State's bid for energy independence. They left, in Gibson's view, a swale of extirpation and death.

This is mountaintop removal mining, the underbelly of the promise of clean, home-grown energy touted by industry and politicians.

No place in the United States has seen the damage and the benefits of mountaintop removal like Appalachia, where one third of the nation's coal is mined. Today about 30 percent of all the coal coming out of the central and southern Appalachians comes via such surface mining.

"There is no such thing as clean coal," Gibson said, talking to a group of journalists under the canopy of his forested knob, where the sylvan sounds of birds and wind carried an undertone of heavy machinery and tumbling rocks.

"I want you folks to write what you see," he said. "And if you write truthfully, you will end one of the most barbaric practices on the planet."

Coal's benefits are considerable: cheap, plentiful energy that simultaneously injects cash into the poorest regions of the country. Coal holds such power that no US administration—Republican or Democrat—has ever tried to stop mountaintop removal.

The full environmental cost is never tallied. No other energy source emits as much carbon dioxide when burned. Coal is so cheap—and so plentiful—that experts generally agree global warming will never be contained until industrialized nations find a way to cap those emissions. And before coal burns, it has to be ripped from the ground.

"Hell's Gate"

Gibson's family has owned this wooded hilltop for 230 years: 50 acres at the end of a rough road, populated with maples, walnuts and a few small houses with tar-paper roofs and kids' swings out in front.

It's a peaceful place, where autumn colors a drizzly autumn morning with red and gold and green. "My mother gave me birth," Gibson often says. "The mountains give me life."

His grandfather discovered in the late 1940s that 426 acres— acreage now being mined—had been stolen away in 1906, after someone filed what Gibson called a fraudulent title showing three "X"s as the signatures of his illiterate forebears.

In 1986 the Princess Beverly Coal Co. dynamited the top off the first ridge of what Gibson said was once his family's forest.

Seven years later Massey Coal offered $140,000 for his hill. He turned them down.

"There should be some things in life money can't buy," he said.

Gibson's water table dropped steadily until 2001, when it disappeared altogether. Today Kayford Mountain has become the iconic face of mountaintop removal mining; Gibson regularly brings groups up to see firsthand what's at stake.

"It amazes me how they can talk about clean coal technology and have an extraction process like this," said Chuck Nelson, a friend and miner who spent 30 years running coal carts underground before he spoke up against mountaintop removal's destruction and lost his job.

He's distressed by the vast scars mountaintop mining leaves in the rugged hills. "What they're destroying can never be fixed. What they're creating is worthless."

What they're creating lies up a rutted road, just beyond a rusty, padlocked pipe blocking the path.

Gibson calls it "Hell's Gate."

"Over here you have life," he said before lifting a leg to trespass. "Over there you have death."

He walks another 100 yards and stops. The point where Gibson stands tops out at 2,400 feet above sea level. The gash below stretches horizon to horizon: Bare rock and earth, where 150-ton dump trucks look like Matchbox toys and big dozers churn the landscape.

That chasm, he says, was once the area's high point, 3,100 feet high. Now it's some 800 feet below him.

"The costs to reclaim this is going out to the people of America," Gibson said.

Stewardship Role

An hour's drive to the east, Andrew Jordon stands on the porch of a hunting shack he had built for his employees and that looks out over a scene of similar desolation.

Except instead of Hell he sees heaven.

Jordon runs a small mining company that is chewing away at 400 acres of the same coal-rich terrain Gibson is trying to keep.

Jordon is the ninth generation of his family to live in that valley. The land he's leasing is owned by the family of a friend and former high school football teammate. His general manager, Rocky Hackworth, is another high school classmate.

"I hunt in these hollows," Jordon said. "To me, it's very important to do it right. Where we're standing today is an area we took down, took the coal out, and put it back to about where it was."

Jordon has been mining for 20 years, has 6,000 acres under lease and has mined and reclaimed 2,200.

For every ton of coal he ships out of his mine, he has to move 28 tons of overburden, or rock. He figures he's pulled 1.5 million tons of coal out so far and has another 6 million tons to go.

Every operation he's started has run into some sort of inherited environmental contamination: a river running at pH 2—fatal to aquatic critters—that Jordon restored to a more natural pH 6. Or a previously botched restoration that his crew reshaped and reforested with black cherry, sugar maple, oak and white ash.

Such work tends to get dropped from press coverage of mountaintop removal, advocates note. Confronting the same group of journalists that had crossed Hell's Gate with Gibson, Coal Association President Bill Raney had to vent a bit of steam: "You say that mining's not protecting the resources," he said. "It drives me nuts when y'all use that same paragraph. It's absolutely meaningless in terms of what we do out here."

Rare Well-Paying Jobs

Jordon's story illustrates another fact of life in coal country every bit as stark as the denuded landscape around Gibson's glade: Poverty.

Median income in the United States was almost $42,000 in 2000, the most recent data the US Census has for nationwide earnings. In the 100 poorest counties—of which 38 lie in Appalachian coal country—the median was half that.

A typical household in Owsley County, in Kentucky's eastern hills, brought home $16,271 in 2000; in McDowell County in West Virginia's southern end, median earnings sat at $16,931.

The median income for a miner in 2000? $44,400, according to the Bureau of Labor Statistics.

"In areas of the country where there are limited education and opportunities, men can live like kings and women can live like queens compared to their neighbors if they mine coal," said LaJuana Wilcher, an attorney with English Lucas Priest & Owsley in Kentucky who was the state's secretary of Environmental and Public Protection from 2003 to 2006.

Coal paid Kentucky $183 million in severance taxes in 2005 and $583 million in other state taxes - almost 10 percent of the state's general fund for that year. That's a lot of highways, hospitals, police officers and schoolrooms for poor states, Wilcher notes.

Big Coal also greases the political rails, contributing $2.6 million through mid-October to both sides in the presidential election, according to the Center for Responsive Politics. Pro-mining West Virginia Gov. Joe Manchin III, a Democrat, crushed his opponents Tuesday.

"This is not a partisan issue," Wilcher said. "You see Sen. (Robert) Byrd (D, W. Va.) and top Republicans all going together on this."

Coal provides direct jobs for 22,000 miners in West Virginia and another 50,000 contractors, according to the Coal Association. It allows men like Jordon and Hackworth to stay in the hills where they grew up. And it feeds the nation's appetite for cheap power.

Miners pulled 377 million tons of coal out of Appalachia in 2007, about a third of the nation's total production. Carbon content varies in coal, but the nation's appetite for the cinder adds 1.8 trillion tons of climate-warming carbon dioxide to the atmosphere annually, according to a 2000 US Energy Information Agency report.

And it's increasing: Industry estimates that 1 billion more tons of coal will be burned worldwide come 2013.

Efforts to reverse that trend quickly run into an immutable wall: Price.

The majority of the country, after all, was against drilling offshore and in the Arctic National Wildlife Refuge last year, Wilcher noted. "And guess what: Gas gets to $4 a gallon, and people wanted to drill offshore for oil and to drill in ANWR."

Raney summed the attitude of many in coal country: "The Lord put the coal in the ground, and everyone up in Boston and elsewhere enjoys using it."

"Stewardship is key," he said. But "should we limit it? Absolutely not."

Replanting the Forest

The growth of mountaintop removal mining can be traced back—as can many an environmental conflict—to efforts to solve another environmental conundrum.

In this case, the need to stem acid rain drove industry out of high-sulfur deposits in northern Appalachia and the Midwest and to the low-sulfur coal of Wyoming's Powder River Basin and the mountains of West Virginia, Kentucky and Tennessee. Many of those Appalachian seams are too shallow to mine conventionally.

The result is that while coal tonnage has decreased in Virginia since 1990, it has stayed steady in central and southern Appalachia as industry compensates with mountaintop removal, said Carl Zipper, director of the Powell River Project, a research program of Virginia Tech aimed at enhancing communities and restoration efforts in the state's coalfields.

There's an incalculable benefit to this shift, noted Wilcher, the lawyer and former regulator: Mountaintop removal mining is safer and requires fewer hands. Coalfield mining deaths have dropped precipitously as a result.

Throughout the '70s an average of 35 miners died annually. By the 1980s the annual death rate had dropped to the mid-20s. Today it's in the single digits; not a single miner died in 2006, a first.

Reclamation practices are changing, too.

In the past, standard practice was to blow the top off the mountain, shovel the overburden into the valley, mine the coal, spray the area with foreign grass seed and hope for the best.

That left the acidic topsoil crucial for forest growth buried under compacted alkaline overburden. Streams became channels. The invasive grass out-competed other plants and stymied any sort of natural succession. Trees, if they were planted, were black locust, ash, sycamore, white pine—far less valuable than the hardwoods they replaced, said Virginia Tech forestry professor Jim Berger.

The Appalachian forest, cleared and logged three times over since Daniel Boone crossed the mountains, would need at least 300 years to grow back at mine sites with such reclamation efforts, Berger figures.

In 2002 the US Army Corps of Engineers changed its restoration guidelines, requiring operators to restore streams in a more natural manner and regulating the type of ripples and pools, sinuosity, slope and conductivity.

The Interior Department's Office of Surface Mining now encourages operators to restore the hardwood forest when they're done, said Patrick Angel, an agency forester and soil scientist based in London, Ky. In every new surface mining permit issued recently in Virginia and in 80 percent of those in West Virginia, the mining company has committed to reclaim the land by planting a diverse hardwood forest, according to agency figures.

Not all rules move reclamation efforts forward, however.

In mid-October the Office of Surface Mining proposed repealing a 25-year-old prohibition on the dumping overburden in valley streams—a repeal the industry describes as crucial for the expansion of mountaintop removal mining.

Environmentalists are aghast. The rule will leave some 350 miles of Appalachian creeks permanently buried, according to the Southern Environmental Law Center, and hydrologists question whether current technology can rebuild healthy streams in the mountains.

Moving on to the Next Mountain

It's unclear what the future holds for Appalachia's hardwood forest or the coal underneath. True, the debate on coal has shifted: Mining advocates acknowledge the industry needs more environmentally friendly technologies to mine and burn it, said Wesleyan College history professor Robert Rupp. "Ten years ago you wouldn't have heard that."

But while President-elect Barack Obama spoke against mountaintop removal during the campaign, key congressional leaders from both parties say they're content with the law as is.

Back on Kayford Mountain, the walnut and hickory and maple trees have all shed their color. On Gibson's front porch, cordwood is stacked neatly for the coming winter, right under a sign saying "Larry's Place—Almost Heaven."

Just over the ridge, miners have started on their next hill. They're awaiting permission to blow the top off Coal River Mountain, where buried seams hold a 14-year supply of coal.

Gibson and his allies say the mountaintop would be an ideal place for wind turbines.

The mining companies say they have no problem with wind power. It'd be a perfect use for the area—after they get the coal out.

Coal Miners Become Solar Technicians

Michael Renner

Michael Renner is a senior researcher at the Worldwatch Institute. His work has principally focused on two topics: the connections between environment and employment (green jobs/green economy), and linkages between the environment and peace and conflict.

Nothing on Earth moves without energy, and most of the energy that people use is of the fossil variety: coal, oil, and natural gas. Although renewable energy is beginning to make inroads, fossil fuels still account for 78 percent of global final energy consumption as of 2014, according to REN21's *Global Status Report 2016*. It is abundantly clear that a fundamental energy makeover is needed if we are to avoid climate chaos—especially with regard to coal, the dirtiest fuel of them all. Until recently, global coal production and use were still growing.

Advocates for renewable energy are typically consumed with matters like technology development, cost competitiveness, and policy support for deploying solar, wind, and other renewables. But the social dimension of the energy transition is just as crucial: in moving away from polluting sources of energy, we need to make sure that the workers who for decades have dug up coal aren't left in the lurch. These are the people who have often paid with their health so that the rest of us could power air conditioners, refrigerators, TVs, and gadgets galore.

Mechanization Takes a Bite

Even before the world decided to get serious about climate policy, not all was well in the world of coal. Communities dependent on coal extraction have been suffering from falling employment for many years, often even as production was rising. This loss of jobs was not the consequence of environmental actions or of a supposed "war on coal" waged by the Obama administration, but the result of growing mechanization, industry restructuring, changing trade patterns, and corporate consolidation.

In the United States—the focus of this piece—coal production peaked in 2008, but employment has been on a downward trajectory for much longer. In mid-2016, just over 55,000 direct mining jobs remained, less than a third of the 174,000 in place 30 years earlier. And these numbers are a far cry from the situation close to a century ago, in 1920, when some 784,000 people worked the mines.

Since the 1970s, there has been an ongoing shift from eastern underground mines in Appalachia to heavily mechanized surface mining operations in Montana and Wyoming. Mines in the latter states can extract more than 10 times as much coal per worker-hour as mines in the Appalachian Basin can. Output from Western basins now surpasses that from the Eastern basins. Coal mining employment in Appalachia was cut in half between 1985 and 1997. Writing in the *Harvard Business Review*, Joshua Pearce notes that, "as coal investors have fled in droves to invest in more profitable companies and industries, [Appalachian] coal workers have been left with pink slips and mortgages on houses with few buyers in blighted coal country."

In the decade to 2014, coal's share of US electricity production fell from just under half to about 39 percent, and more and more capacity is now being retired. This is the result of a number of factors. Coal is under increasing pressure from cheap supplies of natural gas due to the fracking boom and now also from rising supplies of wind and solar electricity. More stringent environmental rules for aging coal plants—almost three-quarters of US coal plants in operation today were built from the 1940s to the 1970s—also play a role. Climate policy is just beginning to make itself felt. These changes reduce coal demand and thus employment at both mines and coal-burning power plants (which, by a rough estimate, represent another 59,000 jobs or so at present). In addition to old plants being shut down, End Coal's Global Coal Plant Tracker lists the cancellation of 41 planned new plants with a combined capacity of about 26 gigawatts (GW).

The Impact of the Clean Power Plan

Through the Clean Power Plan (CPP), the Obama administration is seeking to reduce US power plant emissions to 32 percent below 2005 levels by 2030. (The plan was announced in August 2015, but in February 2016, the Supreme Court stayed implementation pending judicial review.) Each state has been assigned a target for cuts and needs to submit its plans for doing so to the US Environmental Protection Agency (EPA) no later than 2018. Even before the CPP was proposed, coal had dropped from being the leading source of power generation in 32 states in 2000 to dominating in only 20 states in 2015.

In an analysis for the Energy Information Administration, Laura Martin and Jeffrey Jones project that coal plant retirements during 2015–20 as a result of CPP actions may reach 61.6 GW (of a total of 326 GW in operation in 2014), with another 30.4 GW in the 2020s and 7.5 GW in the 2030s. The CPP will thus accelerate the ongoing decline of coal's share in the electricity mix.

The EPA analyzed job impacts under the CPP relative to the likely employment situation in 2020, 2025, and 2030 without the CPP. It concluded that, all in all, job impacts would be positive, in part because clean energy investments are more labor-intensive than fossil fuel investments. Josh Bivens of the Economic Policy Institute expects the largest job gains to come in energy efficiency, although the construction of new natural gas and renewable energy plants also will create substantial jobs. Including indirect effects (supplier and re-spending jobs), by 2020 there could be a net gain of about 360,000 jobs, although this will taper in later years. This doesn't mean that all is well, however: job losses are expected to be geographically concentrated, and few of the workers that will be displaced have a college degree.

A Fair Transition for Workers?

In 2015, the Obama administration initiated the Partnerships for Opportunity and Workforce and Economic Revitalization (POWER) Plus Plan. Under the proposed FY2017 budget, the POWER+ Plan provides $75 million for economic and workforce development strategies in areas affected by changes in the coal economy. This includes $20 million to support dislocated workers (through the Department of Labor), $50 million to communities (through the Appalachian Regional Commission), and another $5 million to communities (through the EPA's Brownfields Program).

The Plan also seeks to strengthen the health care and pension plans of more than 100,000 retired coal miners and their families. The proposed budget further includes $200 million annually over five years for reclamation of abandoned mine lands, linked to job creation strategies. However, in a nod to the coal industry, the POWER+ Plan places a particularly large bet ($2 billion over five years in investment tax credits) on carbon capture and sequestration projects: an expensive boondoggle that would prolong coal use.

Speeding the necessary phase-out of coal use in light of the climate crisis, and taking care of affected workers, will require thinking big. Some audacious proposals have been floated for the US government to simply buy out the entire coal mining industry, shut it down over a number of years, and develop a program with transition payments, relocation assistance, and job-training for workers losing their jobs.

Switching to Solar

For coal miners nearing retirement age, a transition plan could make support payments available until they are eligible to receive their pensions. This is what Germany has done to help thousands of laid-off older coal miners. But younger workers will need—and presumably want—to find new careers. One alternative for displaced coal miners is found in the growing renewable energy sector: specifically, the solar and wind industries.

In a recent study, Edward Louie and Joshua Pearce argue that solar energy growth can, in principle, absorb all US coal workers who will be laid off during the next 15 years. Their study examined occupational patterns, skill sets, and salaries in both industries and found that there are many sufficiently equivalent positions. Following retraining, technical-level workers could expect to earn more in the solar industry than they earned previously in the coal sector, although managers and executives would likely earn less.

To make the switch, education and retraining are essential. In many cases, short courses or on-the-job training might suffice. But individuals seeking engineering and other demanding technical positions will probably need to pursue a multi-year college degree, at considerable cost.

For affected individuals, the cost of retraining could well be significant and, for some, could present an insurmountable financial burden. Under a "fair" transition plan, state or federal governments would establish public retraining programs. (Given the massive subsidies that the coal industry has received over the years, Louie and Pearce suggest that companies should be required to finance a retraining fund—possibly patterned after the 1977 Surface Mining Control and Reclamation Act, which mandates that companies pay into a federal fund for reclamation of abandoned mine land). Nationwide, retraining costs could range from $181 million to $1.9 billion.

Solar and Wind Employment Is Growing

Solar installations are on a steady growth trajectory, which so far has translated into close to 209,000 jobs in the United States, according to the National Solar Jobs Census. Solar manufacturing jobs have largely stagnated at around 30,000 because a substantial share of panel manufacturing takes place abroad (with China being a leading supplier). Most US solar jobs, some 120,000, are installations-related, with another 27,000 in sales and distribution, 26,000 in project development, and about 12,000 in research, government, and other occupations.

The wind industry is longer-established than the solar industry, but it has confronted tremendous swings. Over the years, Congress repeatedly failed to agree on a timely extension of the Production Tax Credit (PTC, the prime support mechanism for wind). This resulted in a rollercoaster for wind capacity additions and employment. In 2013, for example, a 92 percent decline in new installations led to a temporary loss of 30,000 jobs. The current multi-year extension of the PTC to January 2020 permits a steadier path in the next few years.

Overcoming Coal Dependence

The expansion of wind and solar jobs is good news, but there is a reason why out-of-work coal miners aren't necessarily cheering. So far, the bulk of these new jobs are not created in coal country but in other parts of the United States. Reasons for this include varying resource endowments, as well as differences in how strong or weak each state's research, scientific, and industrial base is. A long history of dependence on a coal-based energy system also leaves its signature: "Historically, coal-producing areas have had cheaper power prices and therefore less of a solar market," points out Richard Lawrence, executive director of the North American Board of Certified Energy Professionals.

The expansion of wind and solar jobs is good news, but there is a reason why out-of-work coal miners aren't necessarily cheering. So far, the bulk of these new jobs are not created in coal country but in other parts of the United States. Reasons for this include varying resource endowments, as well as differences in how strong or weak each state's research, scientific, and industrial base is. A long history of dependence on a coal-based energy system also leaves its signature: "Historically, coal-producing areas have had cheaper power prices and therefore less of a solar market," points out Richard Lawrence, executive director of the North American Board of Certified Energy Professionals.

Texas is the only state that is among the top 10 in coal, solar, and wind employment; and Illinois is among the leaders in coal and wind, but not solar. They are thus the only coal states that also have strong employment in clean energy.

A different way to look at the situation is to compare coal employment to combined solar and wind employment. In just nine states—mostly in the Appalachian region, plus Wyoming, Montana, and Alaska—does coal employment exceed solar and wind employment. The problem is particularly pronounced in West Virginia, Kentucky, and Wyoming.

This, of course, is only a snapshot of the current situation and is hardly unalterable. In fact, it is the job of policymakers to bring about an economy that stops destroying the planet's life-support systems AND makes these changes work for people. Federal and state policies can guide, nudge, and encourage a transition toward cleaner energy in parts of the country that have long depended on coal. This can be done with the help of incentives and mandates that build demand for clean energy; strategies to promote regional economic development; and programs to support education and training as needed.

A successful transition requires adequate support over several years. Economic diversification—innovating, persuading companies to relocate and build new facilities, training skilled workers, and establishing an adequate supply chain—is a challenging process, and it may not happen fast enough to create jobs for dislocated coal miners. Therefore, social support measures will play an important role. Transition planning needs to start now, before the full economic impact of climate policy makes itself felt.

CHAPTER 3

Is Nuclear Power the Energy Solution to Climate Change?

Nuclear Energy Is Cleaner than Coal and Natural Gas

Union of Concerned Scientists

The Union of Concerned Scientists puts rigorous, independent science to work to solve our planet's most pressing problems.

E ffectively addressing global warming requires a rapid transformation of the ways in which we produce and consume energy. The scope and impacts of climate change—including rising seas, more damaging extreme weather events, and severe ecological disruption—demand that we consider all possible options for limiting heat-trapping gas emissions—including their respective costs and timelines for implementation.

To help prevent the worst consequences of climate change, the United States must achieve economy-wide net-zero emissions by or before mid-century. The Union of Concerned Scientists (UCS) supports policies and actions that put our nation on the path to attaining this goal.

Swiftly decarbonizing the electric sector, one of the largest sources of US carbon emissions, is among the most cost-effective steps for limiting heat-trapping gas emissions. Renewable energy technologies and energy efficiency measures can help dramatically cut the sector's emissions, and are safe, cost-effective, and commercially available today.

Yet limiting the worst effects of climate change may also require other low- or no-carbon energy solutions, including nuclear power.

Nuclear power produces very few lifecycle carbon emissions. It also faces substantial economic challenges, and carries significant human health and environmental risks. UCS strongly supports

"Nuclear Power & Global Warming," Union of Concerned Scientists. http://www.ucsusa. org/nuclear-power/nuclear-power-and-global-warming#.WfvW_TRx2ih. Reprinted by permission.

policies and measures to strengthen the safety and security of nuclear power.

Nuclear Power and Natural Gas

Today, nuclear power supplies approximately 20 percent of US electricity and is the third largest electricity source in the United States. Most existing US nuclear power plants have licenses that would allow them to operate until the 2030 to 2050 timeframe. However, low natural gas prices, increasingly affordable renewable technologies and grid improvements, declining demand for electricity, and costly age- and safety-related power plant repairs have led to some nuclear reactors being retiring abruptly, with little or no advance planning. Many are being replaced in large part by natural gas.

Though cleaner than coal, natural gas still generates unacceptably large amounts of carbon pollution, especially when the leakage of natural gas from pipelines and other infrastructure is considered. To the extent that a nuclear plant's output is replaced by electricity from natural gas, the resulting emissions set back national efforts to achieve needed emissions reductions.

Today's low market price of natural gas does not reflect the cost that carbon pollution poses to society. UCS strongly supports a robust, economy-wide price on carbon to address this market failure and level the playing field for all low- and no-carbon sources of electricity.

Until carbon pricing is in place, or natural gas prices rise significantly, owners of economically vulnerable nuclear plants will continue asking policymakers for financial assistance. Policymakers facing this situation should consider the cost and feasibility of a range of options, from providing financial support for power plants with strong safety records, to replacing their capacity with renewables, to implementing policies that lower and reconfigure customer demand for electricity. When weighing the various options, policymakers should consider the magnitude and timing of carbon reduction for each option, the respective costs, and the extent to which each option will spur technology innovation.

If policymakers provide financial assistance to existing nuclear plants, they should at the same time strengthen policies such as renewable electricity standards (RES) that stimulate the growth of low-carbon renewable energy as well as energy efficiency programs and policies. Any financial assistance to existing nuclear power plants should not dilute or otherwise come at the expense of incentives for energy efficiency, grid modernization, or renewable resources such as wind and solar, and should include provisions to periodically assess whether continued support is necessary and cost-effective.

Nuclear Power Risks and Impacts

Nuclear power entails substantial safety and security risks, waste disposal challenges, and water requirements. These risks also make nuclear power vulnerable to public rejection (as seen in Japan and Germany following the Fukushima disaster of 2011).

Many of nuclear power's risks can and should be substantially reduced, regardless of whether new nuclear power plants are built. Since its founding, UCS has served as a nuclear safety watchdog, working to ensure that US nuclear power is adequately safe and secure. Our recommendations include better enforcement of existing regulations, expedited transfer of nuclear waste into dry casks, strengthened reactor security requirements, and higher safety standards for new plants. We advocate the continued prohibition of reprocessing and a ban on the use of plutonium-based fuels. We also support continued research and development of nuclear power technologies that are safer, more secure, and lower cost.

Climate Change: The Case For Nuclear Energy

Luis Echavarri

Luis Echavarri is an engineer and former Director General of the OECD Nuclear Energy Agency (NEA).

The Intergovernmental Panel on Climate Change (IPCC) has estimated that to stabilise global temperatures at 2°C above pre-industrial levels–the cut required to avoid catastrophic consequences for the planet–global GHG emissions in 2050 should be reduced by at least 50% below 2000 levels. This could imply reductions of up to 80% by 2050 for OECD countries.

With expected population and energy demand growth, this means reducing the carbon intensity of the world energy system by a factor of four. This is an enormous challenge, and it cannot be faced without mobilising all the available options, including energy conservation and the large-scale deployment of low-carbon energy sources.

No surprise therefore that policy makers from many countries should be expressing a new (or renewed) interest in nuclear energy as a means to address climate change issues. This is because countries producing electricity with nuclear clearly feel they would benefit from carbon emissions savings as nuclear energy substitutes fossil sources. However, nuclear energy was excluded from the two international flexibility mechanisms of the Kyoto Protocol, i.e., the Clean Development Mechanism (CDM) and the Joint Implementation (JI). The upcoming 15th Conference of the Parties (COP-15) to the United Nations Framework Convention on Climate Change (UNFCCC), which will be held on 7-18 December in Copenhagen, will have to discuss in particular the post-Kyoto design of the CDM. This mechanism allows developing countries to receive the benefits for greenhouse gas reductions they achieve on

"Climate change: The case for nuclear energy," by Luis Echavarri, *OECD Observer*, March 2010. Reprinted by permission.

behalf of developed countries with commitments to reductions. It also plays an important role in facilitating foreign direct investment and technology transfer. Given the challenges, this is surely the right moment to take a closer look at the role nuclear energy can play in this context.

Consider greenhouse gas emissions first of all. Throughout the entire nuclear energy chain, from construction to operation and decommissioning, these emissions are negligible compared to their fossil-fuel equivalents, and are comparable with renewable sources such as solar or wind. Furthermore, the GHG emissions of the nuclear chain are mainly due to fossil fuel consumption associated with construction of nuclear power plants, including the likes of cement production, as well as with uranium enrichment. But even these sources are expected to decrease with technological progress. In particular, the deployment of centrifuge technology for enrichment will cut greenhouse gas emissions per unit of nuclear energy produced.

Looked at in terms of equivalent CO_2 emissions per kilowatt hour of energy output, the nuclear chain emits an average of some 8 g CO_2-eq./kWh, while the gas chain (assuming use of the combined-cycle technology) emits around 400 g CO_2-eq./kWh and the coal chain with state-of-the-art power plants emits around 1,000 g CO_2-eq./kWh. Carbon capture and sequestration could drastically reduce the emissions of coal-fired power plants; however, this is not yet a mature and competitive technology. Most renewable energy chains for electricity generation emit between 5 and 60 g CO_2-eq./kWh, hydropower being on the lower side of the range and photovoltaic sources on the higher side.

Nuclear energy already contributes to lower carbon emissions in the world's economies, especially in OECD countries where it provides more than 20% of total electricity supply. It has been estimated that, since the commercial development of nuclear electricity generation, the cumulative savings of CO_2 emissions as a result of nuclear power plants substituting for coal-fired units is around 60 Gt CO_2-eq., representing some 20% of the cumulated emissions of the power sector during that period. At present, the emissions avoided thanks to nuclear electricity generation are around 2 Gt CO_2-eq. per year assuming that electricity from nuclear energy would be substituted by other technologies in proportion to their current share in the energy mix. That means nuclear energy helps "decarbonise" the economy. In fact, in OECD countries, the GHG emissions from the energy sector would increase by one-third if nuclear power plants are shut down and replaced by fossil-fuelled power plants.

With the ongoing process of plant life extension, the existing global fleet–439 reactors as of June 2008–will continue producing carbon-free electricity for several decades and the reactors under construction–around 50 at present around the world–will add scores of gigawatts to installed nuclear capacity by 2015. In many OECD countries, however, concrete steps towards ordering and building new nuclear power plants have not yet been taken. In short, most energy scenarios show only a moderate increase in installed nuclear capacity worldwide in spite of the repeated announcements of a nuclear revival.

The Nuclear Energy Agency projects that in 2050, nuclear capacity worldwide could range between 540 and 1400 GWe, compared with 370 GWe today. Under the high scenario, the share of nuclear energy in total electricity generation would reach 22%, i.e., 7% more than in 2008, but in the low scenario it would be only 9%, i.e., 6% less than in 2008. The annual savings of CO_2 emissions that would result from these low and high nuclear scenarios amount to some 4.5 and 11.5 Gt CO_2-eq. respectively. These quantities are not at all negligible and, in the high scenario, would contribute massively to reaching CO_2 reductions identified by the IPCC in its business as usual scenarios.

More rapid deployment of nuclear energy could improve on this scenario, and is achievable from the technical, industrial and financial viewpoints, but would require stronger political and social support.

This also means overcoming some of the main challenges to its further development. It is high time the nuclear industry and governments addressed the legitimate public concerns about radioactive waste disposal for instance, as well as reinforcing safeguards in non-proliferation agreements. In addition, the financial risks of nuclear projects need to be discussed openly. Like other low-carbon technologies such as renewables, the cost structure of nuclear energy is characterised by high capital costs and low variable costs, which can be a disadvantage in liberalised power markets with volatile prices. On the other hand, nuclear energy has the advantage that its average costs over the full life cycle of the plant are highly competitive. Suitable financing models and government support can address the question of capital costs for nuclear as well as for other low-carbon technologies.

The challenge to reduce carbon emissions cannot be overstated. It is now time to recognise the value of nuclear energy for reducing greenhouse gas emissions in the legal and institutional framework to be developed at Copenhagen and beyond. This would provide the impetus needed to deal with the challenges and realise the full potential of nuclear energy as a reliable part of our energy and environmental future.

Nuclear Energy Innovation Fights Climate Change

The International Atomic Energy Agency

The International Atomic Energy Agency is the world's central intergovernmental forum for scientific and technical co-operation in the nuclear field. It works for the safe, secure, and peaceful uses of nuclear science and technology, contributing to international peace and security and the United Nations' Sustainable Development Goals.

[...]

The latest report of the Intergovernmental Panel on Climate Change (IPCC) presents a large volume of new evidence that the climate system of the Earth is changing owing to increasing concentrations of greenhouse gases (GHGs), especially carbon dioxide (CO_2), resulting from emissions from human activities, mainly the burning of fossil fuels and land use change. Global mean surface temperatures are increasing; precipitation volumes and spatial and temporal distribution patterns are changing; the oceans are warming and the sea level is rising; features of extreme weather and climate events are changing.

The 2015 Paris Agreement of the United Nations Framework Convention on Climate Change (UNFCCC) intends to lessen the distressing impacts of climate change on ecological and socioeconomic systems and to modify current emissions rates to the lowest possible levels by setting an objective of limiting the increase in the global average temperature from pre-industrial levels to significantly less than 2°C. Current policies and investment trends for low carbon technologies fall short of delivering the needed reduction in GHG emissions. Intended Nationally Determined Contributions to GHG emission reduction, communicated by the parties to the UNFCCC before the Paris Agreement, form

IAEA publication: International Atomic Energy Agency Climate Change and Nuclear Power 2016, IAEA, Vienna (2016). Reproducing the extracts with permission by the IAEA.

an important base upon which to build ambitions for mitigation. Power generation from low carbon sources, including nuclear energy, is a critical pillar in meeting the objectives of the UNFCCC.

Energy is a fundamental prerequisite for social and economic development. Mainly driven by large, fast growing, emerging economies, global primary energy demand is projected to increase to nearly 18 gigatonnes of oil equivalent (Gtoe) by 2040 according to the New Policies Scenario of the International Energy Agency (IEA) of the Organisation for Economic Co-operation and Development (OECD). Without the much stronger incentives to decarbonize global energy systems that are reflected in the New Policies Scenario (but which have not yet been implemented), energy related CO_2 emissions are projected to rise by 16% by 2040. By contrast, meeting the 2°C target entails a 41% reduction in total energy related CO_2 emissions and a 70% reduction in power sector emissions. The pace of addressing CO_2 emissions from the energy sector differs in every country, depending on its level of economic development, access to best-in-class technologies, availability of cheap domestic fossil resources and renewable energy potential, access to finance and on the existence of policies and standards already in place or proposed, for instance, in Intended Nationally Determined Contributions.

Nuclear power is among the energy sources and technologies available today that could help meet the climate–energy challenge. GHG emissions from nuclear power plants (NPPs) are negligible, and nuclear power, together with hydropower and wind based electricity, is among the lowest GHG emitters when emissions over the entire life cycle are considered, standing at less than 15 grams CO_2-equivalent (g CO_2-eq) per kW·h (kilowatt-hour).

The historical role played by NPPs in the decarbonization of the global electricity mix extends to the future: in the New Policies Scenario, more than 3 Gt CO_2 would be avoided in the power sector in 2040 owing to the expansion of nuclear capacity worldwide (2Gt CO_2 was avoided by nuclear power in 2013). The role of nuclear power is expected to be even larger in scenarios consistent with the 2°C target (more than double current capacity levels by 2050), depending on assumptions about the relative costs and performance of other low carbon technologies. There is also significant scope for innovation in advanced and revolutionary designed reactors as well as in small modular reactors to advance the role of nuclear energy in addressing climate change and sustainable development.

A number of challenges need to be overcome to enable large scale nuclear power generation capacity in a country. Historical experience in the industry has demonstrated that it is possible to succeed, regardless of sociopolitical systems and the stage of economic development that a country may be at. When nuclear investments start to increase, manufacturing and construction capacities expand to meet the need. Financing nuclear power investments would also be feasible given stable government policies, proper regulatory regimes and risk allocation schemes. Once built, nuclear plants usually have very low running costs and tend to earn high margins in most electricity markets.

The scale of nuclear ambition in future updates of Intended Nationally Determined Contributions, which represent a progression towards the objectives of the Paris Agreement, will also affect the timely deployment of nuclear power. In the next couple of years, the rules and modalities of a new market mechanism (established under the Paris Agreement to be used by the parties to contribute to the mitigation of GHG emissions and to support sustainable development), will be determined. It is important that the nuclear power option be kept open under this mechanism for parties that wish to include it and thereby increase their options and the flexibility and cost effectiveness of their climate change mitigation strategies.

The policies supporting the transition to a low carbon economy will only prove effective if implemented jointly with other objectives to maintain a secured supply of energy and meet other sustainable development goals, to avoid potentially inefficient and conflicting outcomes. Nuclear energy can contribute to resolving energy supply concerns. Despite significant decreases in fossil fuel prices in recent years, fears of a return to previous highs and concerns about the security of supply from politically unstable regions are continuous considerations in the energy strategies of many countries. Including nuclear power in the energy supply mix can help alleviate these concerns because ample uranium resources are available from reliable sources throughout the world, and the cost of uranium remains a small fraction of the total cost of nuclear electricity. Besides the reliability and predictability that nuclear power offers in the electricity markets, it also has non-climatic environmental benefits and minimizes the impact on human health as it emits practically no local or regional air pollutants. Among the power generation technologies, it has one of the lowest external costs in terms of damage to human health and the environment that are not accounted for in the price of electricity.

Concerns about nuclear energy relating to radiation risks, waste management, safety and proliferation still exist and influence public acceptance. Radiation risks from normal plant operation remain low, at a level that is virtually indistinguishable from natural and medical sources of public radiation exposure. Thus, NPPs remain one of the safest industrial sectors for their workers and for the public at large owing to concerted efforts by operators of nuclear facilities and by international organizations such as the IAEA. NPPs incorporate redundant safety systems, and their operation is characterized by industry commitments to safety, international safety coordination, extensive training and stringent qualifications for nuclear workers, and effective responses to accidents. Institutional arrangements are being improved and further technological solutions sought to prevent the diversion of nuclear material for non-peaceful purposes. Spent fuel has been safely stored since nuclear power first generated electricity for public consumption in 1954. Geological and other scientific foundations for the safe disposal of spent nuclear fuel and high level waste are well established. The first repositories are expected to start operation within a decade. Public acceptance, although slowly recovering in some countries, still needs time to rebound to the level of support seen before the Fukushima Daiichi accident. The nuclear sector needs to improve further and to provide adequate responses to these concerns in order to realize its full potential.

Investment in nuclear power is also associated with activities in other sectors in the economy, such as construction, manufacturing and services, as well as with employment creation, and thus it contributes to overall economic growth. Recent experience in countries with developed nuclear power programmes showed that in terms of labour market effects, secondary or "ripple" effects, though indirect, might be much higher than the magnitude of direct employment. A balanced view on benefits and concerns underpins the need to assess the net effects on the society from investments in any energy technologies, including nuclear technology. Subject to a country's overall economic and social policy objectives, the implementation of the Paris Agreement, together with the 2030 Sustainable Development Agenda, may provide additional incentives for nuclear programme development.

Climate change mitigation is one of the salient reasons for considering nuclear power in future national energy portfolios. Where, when, by how much and under what arrangements nuclear power will contribute to climate change mitigation will depend on local conditions, national priorities and on international arrangements. The final decision to introduce, use, expand or phase out nuclear energy in a national energy portfolio rests with sovereign States.

[...]

Role of Nuclear Innovation in Climate Change Mitigation

An important outcome from COP21 and the Paris Agreement is that innovation is absolutely critical "for an effective, long-term global response to climate change and promoting economic growth and sustainable development." Innovation, in this context, implies not only the use of new technologies but also creative approaches to implementing actions and regulations, and creating business models. Several conference speakers amplified this message. For example, Ernest Moniz, Secretary of Energy, United States of America, was reported to have particularly insisted on the virtuous circle of increasing innovation, reducing costs and increasing the deployment of low carbon technologies.

Fatih Birol, the Executive Director of the IEA, said, "Innovation is at the heart of fighting climate change", while Maroš Sefčovič, EU vice president, noted that "it will be important for the future to look into how we can streamline and synergise existing efforts to create truly global collaboration in energy technology innovation".

The clear message is that innovation, together with investment and research in cleaner and sustainable technologies and strategies, rather than continued subsidies for polluting activities, is necessary to bend the carbon emissions curve downward.

A given country's level of research, development and demonstration [RD&D] is seen as a key indicator of its capacity for innovation. Investments in RD&D also attract and stimulate national investments and efforts in innovation including in low carbon technologies. Between 2015 and 2030, more than US $400 billion/year needs to be invested in low carbon power supply, including US $81 billion/year in nuclear (see Section 2.2). The Lima–Paris Action Agenda's focus on innovation is supported by pledges made at COP21 under Mission Innovation including 20 countries seeking to double public investment in RD&D between 2015 and 2020. Investments are needed to support transformational clean energy technologies that can be scaled to the economic and market conditions of a country. These currently amount to about US $10 billion/ year. Countries expect that all clean energy technologies, including nuclear and carbon capture, can be driven to expansion and success through innovation.

Private capital investments in clean energy were initiated through the launch of the Breakthrough Energy Coalition. This includes 28 major investors from 10 countries pledging to invest extraordinary levels of private capital in early stage innovations. Investments are guided by a set of principles to catalyse broad business participation in the commercialization and deployment of clean energy technologies worldwide. Current contributors include active supporters of innovative nuclear designs and nuclear energy development, most notably Bill Gates' clean energy investment in TerraPower, an innovative fourth generation reactor design.

At the COP21, climate scientists (James Hansen, Tom Wigley, Ken Caldeira and Kerry Emanuel) suggested that only a combined strategy employing all major sustainable clean energy options— including renewables and nuclear power—would suffice to reduce carbon emissions enough to meet climate goals. According to the scientists, innovation is pivotal for the expansion of nuclear power. It is needed in design for constructability, disposability and sustainability, as well as in project management and standardization within the nuclear supply chain to strengthen its economic attractiveness. Innovation would make nuclear power more socially accepted and its benefits would be better realized: for the climate, because it is a low carbon technology, to health and the environment because it is non-polluting, and for system costs because it offers power generation with less need for grid enhancements. Additionally, there are enough opportunities for technical innovation for current and future generations of nuclear reactors.

The continued operation of current nuclear technologies is important for achieving short term reductions in GHG emissions from the power sector, given the urgency of climate mitigation. Current commercial power reactors (Generation II) already avoid 2 Gt CO_2/year and innovations can help these reactors to run longer. Advancements are needed for performance upgrades to extend the useful life (long term operation) of existing reactors, and performance and safety upgrades also need to be certified for life extensions. Additionally, concerns about final waste storage, nuclear proliferation risks, cost uncertainties and nuclear safety must be addressed. New builds of advanced reactors (Generation

III) and evolutionary reactors (Generation III+) are needed to replace up to 77% of the current reactors retiring by 2050 and to expand nuclear in some markets (for example, in Asia). These new reactors need to overcome barriers to bringing the technology to market including: obtaining financial assistance, access to facilities to conduct necessary RD&D activities, construction of demonstrators and prototypes, and certification and licensing of new nuclear reactor concepts. First-of-a-kind advanced reactors under construction or in early operation need to be optimized through innovation, in order to dramatically reduce licensing and construction costs and to demonstrate their safety capabilities.

Small modular reactors (SMRs) are expected to be deployed with enhanced safety systems in the next 10–20 years. They are envisioned to provide a nuclear low carbon alternative to countries without large power grids, less developed infrastructures and limited financing capabilities. The technology also aims to reduce costs through modularization and factory construction thus reducing construction times. The SMRs are better suited for deployment in remote areas and may additionally support non-electrical applications such as sea water desalination, district heating and heat for low temperature processes such as biomass drying.

Future revolutionary (Generation IV) reactors can expand nuclear energy over the longer term (2030+). Designs for these reactors include molten salt reactors, supercritical water cooled reactors, very high temperature reactors and fast reactors. The very high temperature reactors may be used in the future to produce hydrogen and support petrochemical and other industrial applications. Fast reactors (e.g. molten salt reactors and accelerator driven systems) could derive significant energy from used fuel to reduce the need for mining and enrichment, which are the most CO_2 intensive steps in the nuclear fuel cycle. Fast reactors specially configured to burn used fuel can substantially reduce the long lived radionuclides in the waste products and the volume of waste requiring deep geological disposal. Current RD&D plans for these systems are contained in the Generation IV technology roadmap.

Innovations in the nuclear fuel cycle are also needed to support all generations of nuclear reactors. New fuel designs are needed to support future operating conditions (e.g. load-following), longer fuel cycles and higher burnups. Innovations are needed in the separation and recycling of nuclear materials to fuel future Generation IV fast reactors. Research on thorium could help to extend geological resources for nuclear fuels to meet growing energy demands in regions where uranium is not available.

Ultimately, nuclear fusion is the technology at the cutting edge of nuclear RD&D and innovation. Fusion eliminates the production of long lived radioactive waste and the fuel is produced from abundant material such as water, eliminating problems such as energy resource scarcity and nuclear proliferation concerns.

The priorities for investing in nuclear RD&D need to include the full scope of activity (prototypes and reactors, fuel cycle/waste management and innovative energy systems). Several national and international initiatives have recently been initiated in response to growing energy demands and the global imperative raised at COP21 to address climate change:

- China intends to generate up to 10% of its power from nuclear energy (110 nuclear reactors) as part of a pledge to the international community to reduce carbon emissions and to increase the share of non-fossil fuels in primary energy consumption to around 20% by 2030. China stresses the role of innovation, safety and the popularization of its technologies.
- The United States of America launched the Gateway for Accelerated Innovation in Nuclear programme in 2016 in response to the Paris Agreement to enhance the deployment of innovative nuclear technology to the market. It will provide the nuclear energy community with access to the technical, regulatory and financial infrastructures necessary

to move new or advanced nuclear reactor designs towards commercialization while ensuring the continued safe, reliable, and economic operation of the existing nuclear fleet.

- The UK's National Nuclear Laboratory established the Nuclear Innovation and Research Office to provide advice to Government, industry and other bodies on R&D and innovation opportunities in the nuclear sector. According to reports, the "UK would double funding for the Department of Energy and Climate Change's energy innovation programme to £500 million over five years, which will help pay for an ambitious nuclear research programme that will revive the country's nuclear expertise and help turn it into a leader in SMR technology."

- The European Union Horizon 2020 advances nuclear research and training activities through the European Atomic Energy Community's (EURATOM) work programme. The emphasis is on continually improving nuclear safety, security and radiation protection, to contribute to the long term decarbonization of the energy system in a safe, efficient and secure way. The focus is on nuclear fission, including the safety and feasibility of innovative reactors and closed fuel cycle options, radiation protection and nuclear fusion.

- The OECD Nuclear Energy Agency launched Nuclear Innovation 2050 to define which technologies are necessary to achieve the nuclear growth needed for the Paris Agreement, and what RD&D is needed versus what is actually being done. A roadmap of RD&D until 2100 will be developed to address the gaps and timelines for five categories: reactors, fuel/fuel cycle, waste/decommissioning, emerging energy systems and cross-cutting issues.

There are many opportunities for innovation to advance nuclear energy in addressing climate change. Steps are being actively taken as a result of the Paris Agreement to ensure a continued role for nuclear energy. Although the level of investment in RD&D needs to be increased to meet this challenge, the added cost is justified by continued avoidance of CO_2 emissions with low carbon energy serving increasing rates of electrification throughout the world, and by the extension of nuclear technology beyond the power sector into non-electric applications.

[…]

Nuclear Energy Is a Safe and Smart Strategy

The Nuclear Energy Agency

The Nuclear Energy Agency (NEA) is an intergovernmental agency that facilitates cooperation among countries with advanced nuclear technology infrastructures to seek excellence in nuclear safety, technology, science, environment, and law.

The global response to address climate change is a key policy challenge of the 21st century. Many governments around the world have agreed that action should be taken to achieve large cuts in greenhouse gas (GHG) emissions over the coming decades, to adapt to the impacts of climate change and to ensure the necessary financial and technical support for developing countries to take action. They are working towards an international agreement to achieve these goals under the United Nations Framework Convention on Climate Change (UNFCCC), which organises annual Conferences of the Parties (COP). COP 21 will be held in Paris on 30 November to 11 December 2015. There is a growing scientific consensus that global annual GHG emissions will need to be reduced by at least 50% from today's levels by 2050 if the world is to limit the average temperature increase to 2°C by the end of the century in order to avoid the worst consequences of global warming.

Not all anthropogenic greenhouse gas emissions are due to the extraction, transformation and consumption of energy. Sectors such as agriculture and industry also contribute through specific processes. However, energy use is responsible for about 70% of all GHG emissions, a share that has remained roughly stable, although absolute emissions have been increasing. The need to cut GHG emissions has therefore become a major driver of energy policy. The main gases emitted by the energy sector are nitrous oxide

OECD/NEA (2015), "Nuclear Energy: Combating Climate Change," https://www.oecd-nea.org/ndd/pubs/2015/7208-climate-change-2015.pdf. Reprinted by permission.

(N_2O), methane (CH_4) and carbon dioxide (CO_2). Of the three, carbon dioxide is by far the most important, contributing over 90% of total energy-related greenhouse gas emissions and about two-thirds of total greenhouse gas emissions. In the energy sector, CO_2 is exclusively generated by fossil fuel combustion. Moving away from the consumption of fossil fuels such as coal, oil and gas towards low-carbon sources such as nuclear, hydro or renewables is therefore a key strategy for reducing climate change and risk.

In the past 30 years, carbon emissions have been steadily rising due to the increased use of all three fossil fuels: coal, oil and gas and these now stand at 32 Gigatonnes (Gt). The only periods in history when emissions dipped were during the economic crisis in former Soviet Union countries at the beginning of the 1990s and after the global economic crisis in 2008. It is interesting to note, however, that 2014 was the first year in which global carbon emissions did not increase in the absence of a major economic crisis, although growth in the People's Republic of China has slowed. In 2013, coal contributed 44% of global energy-related CO_2 emissions, oil contributed 35% and gas 20%. The contribution of coal in meeting total global energy demand was 29%, that of oil was 31% and that of gas 21%. The remaining 18% of total energy demand was met by carbon-free sources of energy such as hydropower, renewable energies and nuclear energy (IEA, 2014b).

[...]

Can Nuclear Power Be Expanded Rapidly Enough to Make a Full Contribution to Combating Climate Change?

Nuclear power technology has been developing continuously over more than 50 years, and the latest designs for nuclear plants— generation III plants—incorporate the experience gained over these decades in terms of safety, fuel performance and efficiency. While further technological development can be expected, nuclear power is already a mature technology. The barriers to its more rapid deployment are essentially political, social and financial, rather than technical.

Before significant nuclear power expansion can begin in any country, clear and sustained policy support from governments is needed, as part of an overall strategy to address the challenges of providing secure and affordable energy supplies while protecting the environment, both in terms of GHG emissions and air pollution. In recent years, a number of governments have reassessed their approach to nuclear energy and now view it as an important part of their energy strategy, while others continue to believe that nuclear should not be part of their energy supply mix.

The 2°C scenario presented in the previous section projects more than a doubling of the current nuclear capacity of 390 GW today to 930 GW by 2050. This would require annual grid connection rates of over 12 GW in the present decade, rising to well above 20 GW in the following decade. However, current grid connection rates are far below these targets, with annual rates between 3 and 5 GW per year since 2010. A comparison with the major expansion of nuclear power in the 1970s and 1980s indicates that, given strong policy support, nuclear power could expand in a sufficiently rapid manner. During the 1970s, nuclear reactor construction projects typically reached 30 per year, peaking even at above 40. This was translated later to annual grid connection rates from 15 and 30 GW between 1980 and 1987, much higher rates than today's. At the beginning of the 1980s, there were 180 reactors under construction in the world, compared to fewer than 70 today. Although these were smaller than many current designs, the technology was also less well developed at that time. In addition, relatively few countries were involved in that expansion, and overall global industrial capacity was much smaller.

The two most important challenges of building a new nuclear power plant today are assembling the conditions for successful financing and managing a highly complex construction process. Because of their high fixed costs, nuclear power plants fare better with stable long-term prices. High fixed costs of investment are common to all low-carbon technologies such as nuclear power, but also hydropower, wind or solar PV. In markets with price risk, nuclear power is at a competitive disadvantage with fossil fuel-based technologies such as gas or coal, even though it scores as well or better on traditional measures of competitiveness such as average levelised costs of electricity (LCOE).

While a robust carbon price would certainly be helpful to decarbonise electricity systems, measures ensuring price stability such as long-term contracts, regulated tariffs, feed-in tariffs (FITs) or contracts for difference (CfD) remain important for all low- carbon generating projects including nuclear power. All successful projects rely on long-term financing. However, for the time being such long-term nancing is still based on individual, ad hoc measures rather than on a general investment framework capable of spurring nuclear power growth on a broader basis. This would include a rethink of electricity market design. There are no technology-neutral electricity market designs. The competitiveness of nuclear power will be very different in liberalised electricity markets than in regulated markets.

In construction, where the emergence of a competitive, global supply chain is not yet ensured, the convergence of nuclear engineering codes and quality standards remains a key step to promote both competition and public confidence. In parallel, a number of smaller technological and managerial improvements keep the industry moving forward.

During a time of major technological, structural and geographical shifts, it is important that the global nuclear industry maintains a dynamic of continuous technological, logistical and managerial improvement. There is good reason to be optimistic that given sufficiently stable framework conditions, the nuclear industry will be able to deliver on its contribution to combating climate change and reducing global greenhouse gas emissions.

Will Uranium Supplies Be Adequate?

A major expansion of nuclear power would require a commensurate increase in nuclear fuel cycle capacities. Nuclear power has a relatively complex fuel cycle, involving uranium mining as well as several industrial processes to prepare the finished fuel assemblies, which, for most reactor types, consist of pellets of enriched uranium dioxide encased in a lattice of metallic tubes. Expanding the use of nuclear power will require increased uranium production, as well as the associated uranium enrichment capacities. Given sufficient time, both production and enrichment should increase to levels that would allow for the fuelling of a deployment of nuclear power plants as ambitious as that projected in the 2DS of the IEA/NEA *Nuclear Roadmap: Nuclear Energy*.

Uranium mining has been affected by a prolonged period of low prices, which lasted throughout the 1990s and only ended in 2003. Reasons for these lower prices included lower than expected nuclear power expansion and past overproduction with the market entry of large stocks of previously mined uranium held by utilities and governments, including former military stocks released through nuclear disarmament following the end of the Cold War. In 2003, uranium prices began to increase, eventually rising to levels not seen since the 1980s, then rising more rapidly through 2005 and 2006 with spot prices reaching a peak through 2007 and 2008, then falling off rapidly. The Fukushima Daiichi accident precipitated an initially rapid decline in prices that has continued more gradually through to the end of 2013 as reactors were shut down in Germany and gradually laid-up in Japan when the new nuclear safety regime was established. Projects to increase uranium production, implemented before the accident, resulted in increasing production even as demand weakened and the market became saturated with supply, putting further downward pressure on prices through to the end of 2013.

According to the 2014 edition of *Uranium: Resources, Production and Demand* (the "Red Book") (NEA/IAEA, 2014), annual uranium production in 2013 was balanced with annual requirements for the first time since the early 1990s, due to both an increase in production and decreased requirements linked to a great extent to post- Fukushima permanent or temporary shutdowns. Total identified resources at a cost of less than USD 130 per kg of uranium have increased by almost 11% since 2011. Today, there is more than 100 years of supply at current rates of consumption, though investments in mines will continue to be needed. Current identified resources are also sufficient to meet higher growth in nuclear generation. In its high case, the Red Book projects 680 GW in 2035, which is close to the 720 GW projected in the IEA's 2DS for the same period.

Even if today over 90% of the world's uranium output is produced by only eight countries, resources are widespread around the world. Furthermore, the nature of the nuclear fuel cycle means that nuclear power plants are not dependent on continuous deliveries of large quantities of fuel. Nuclear fuel is a very concentrated energy source and is easy to stockpile, which explains why many governments view nuclear power as an important component of their strategy to increase the security of their energy supplies.

In the longer run, nuclear fuel also offers important possibilities for recycling, since with current water- cooled reactors, only a small fraction of the uranium is usually consumed in the reactor. This could vastly increase the energy potential of existing uranium stocks and known resources, from a few hundred to several thousand years of nuclear fuel demand. It could also greatly reduce the radiotoxicity of the resulting high-level waste (HLW). Present recycling techniques use sensitive technologies, and are unlikely to expand significantly in the short to medium term. However, the expansion of recycling in the longer term could be facilitated by further technological development of recycling technologies, and the deployment of fast neutron reactors, one of the generation IV reactor technologies currently being developed. Such deployment of advanced technologies would have important implications for the long-term sustainability of nuclear energy, as it could multiply by between 30 to 60 times, and perhaps more, the amount of energy extracted from each tonne of uranium, thereby making available uranium resources sufficient to power fast neutron reactors for several thousands of years.

Safety, Radioactive Waste Management, and Non-Proliferation

Low-level and short-lived intermediate-level wastes account for the largest volumes of radioactive waste, although they only contain a small proportion of its total radioactivity. Technologies for the disposal of such waste are well developed and most countries with major nuclear programmes operate facilities for their disposal or are at an advanced stage in developing them. Governments should continue to work with the nuclear industry to ensure the safe management and disposal of nuclear waste.

Most of the radioactivity generated by nuclear power plant operation is concentrated in the smaller volumes of HLW, which comprise spent nuclear fuel and waste from recycling, for countries that have chosen that strategy. There is, in fact, no immediate requirement to dispose of such materials as they can be safely and easily stored in existing facilities for many years. Nevertheless, countries with existing nuclear programmes are developing longer-term plans for the final disposal of waste, and there is an international consensus that deep geological disposal of HLW is the most technically feasible and safe solution. Although no facilities for final disposal of such waste are yet in operation, some countries are moving ahead to license, construct and operate deep geological repositories (DGRs). Finland and Sweden will have DGRs in operation in the early 2020s and France after 2025.

The safety performance of nuclear power plants and other civil nuclear facilities in OECD countries is generally excellent, certainly by comparison with other energy cycles. Reactors of the latest designs have enhanced safety features and systems, including increased levels of "passive" safety and systems to prevent and mitigate severe accidents. Following the Fukushima

Daiichi accident in Japan in March 2011, safety requirements were enhanced for all nuclear operators and hazard re-evaluations or "stress tests" were carried out for all operating nuclear power plants, as well as for reactors under construction. Improvements in areas such as seismic resistance, emergency power supply and decay heat removal systems were recommended in many cases and are in the process of being implemented by operators.

A major expansion of nuclear power would mean nuclear power plants being built in countries without previous experience in nuclear regulation. It is essential therefore that these newcomer countries develop appropriate legal and institutional frameworks, including a strong and independent regulatory system. The International Atomic Energy Agency (IAEA) is engaging with many such countries to develop their institutional capabilities in this regard.

At the same time, it is important to point out that materials or technologies developed for civil use in electricity production could potentially be diverted for military purposes. The IAEA safeguards system and Treaty on the Non-Proliferation of Nuclear Weapons (commonly known as the Non-Proliferation Treaty or NPT) have served well in helping to prevent a diversion of civil nuclear materials and technologies. However, a major expansion of nuclear power, involving many more countries, is likely to require a strengthening of the non- proliferation regime and its implementation. A balance needs to be found between achieving non-proliferation goals and providing adequate supply assurances to countries relying on nuclear power.

[…]

Nuclear Waste Is Dirty and Dangerous

Union of Concerned Scientists

The Union of Concerned Scientists puts rigorous, independent science to work to solve our planet's most pressing problems.

Reprocessing is a series of chemical operations that separates plutonium and uranium from other nuclear waste contained in the used (or "spent") fuel from nuclear power reactors. The separated plutonium can be used to fuel reactors, but also to make nuclear weapons. In the late 1970's, the United States decided on nuclear non-proliferation grounds not to reprocess spent fuel from US power reactors, but instead to directly dispose of it in a deep underground geologic repository where it would remain isolated from the environment for at least tens of thousands of years.

While some supporters of a US reprocessing program believe it would help solve the nuclear waste problem, reprocessing would not reduce the need for storage and disposal of radioactive waste. Worse, reprocessing would make it easier for terrorists to acquire nuclear weapons materials, and for nations to develop nuclear weapons programs.

Reprocessing Would Increase the Risk of Nuclear Terrorism

Less than 20 pounds of plutonium is needed to make a simple nuclear weapon. If the plutonium remains bound in large, heavy, and highly radioactive spent fuel assemblies (the current US practice), it is nearly impossible to steal. In contrast, separated plutonium is not highly radioactive and is stored in a concentrated powder form. Some claim that new reprocessing technologies that would leave the plutonium blended with other elements, such as

"Nuclear Reprocessing: Dangerous, Dirty, and Expensive," Union of Concerned Scientists. http://www.ucsusa.org/nuclear-power/nuclear-plant-security/nuclear-reprocessing#. WfwHV7Wjfcs. Reprinted by permission.

neptunium, would result in a mixture that would be too radioactive to steal. This is incorrect; neither neptunium nor the other elements under consideration are radioactive enough to preclude theft. Most of these other elements are also weapon-usable.

Moreover, commercial-scale reprocessing facilities handle so much of this material that it has proven impossible to keep track of it accurately in a timely manner, making it feasible that the theft of enough plutonium to build several bombs could go undetected for years.

A US reprocessing program would add to the worldwide stockpile of separated and vulnerable civil plutonium that sits in storage today, which totaled roughly 250 metric tons as of the end of 2009—enough for some 30,000 nuclear weapons. Reprocessing the US spent fuel generated to date would increase this by more than 500 metric tons.

Reprocessing Would Increase the Ease of Nuclear Proliferation

US reprocessing would undermine the US goal of halting the spread of fuel cycle technologies that are permitted under the Nuclear Non-Proliferation Treaty but can be used to make nuclear weapons materials. The United States cannot credibly persuade other countries to forgo a technology it has newly embraced for its own use. Although some reprocessing advocates claim that new reprocessing technologies under development will be "proliferation resistant," they would actually be more difficult for international inspectors to safeguard because it would be harder to make precise measurements of the weapon-usable materials during and after processing. Moreover, all reprocessing technologies are far more proliferation-prone than direct disposal.

Reprocessing Would Hurt US Nuclear Waste Management Efforts

First, there is no spent fuel storage crisis that warrants such a drastic change in course. Hardened interim storage of spent fuel in dry casks is an economically viable and secure option for at least fifty years.

Second, reprocessing does not reduce the need for storage and disposal of radioactive waste, and a geologic repository would still be required. Plutonium constitutes only about one percent of the spent fuel from US reactors. After reprocessing, the remaining material will be in several different waste forms, and the total volume of nuclear waste will have been increased by a factor of twenty or more, including low-level waste and plutonium-contaminated waste. The largest component of the remaining material is uranium, which is also a waste product because it is contaminated and undesirable for reuse in reactors. Even if the uranium is classified as low-level waste, new low-level nuclear waste facilities would have to be built to dispose of it. And to make a significant reduction in the amount of high-level nuclear waste that would require disposal, the used fuel would need to be reprocessed and reused many times with an extremely high degree of efficiency—an extremely difficult endeavor that would likely take centuries to accomplish.

Finally, reprocessing would divert focus and resources from a US geologic disposal program and hurt—not help—the US nuclear waste management effort. The licensing requirements for the reprocessing, fuel fabrication, and waste processing plants would dwarf those needed to license a repository, and provide additional targets for public opposition. What is most needed today is a renewed focus on secure interim storage of spent fuel and on gaining the scientific and technical consensus needed to site a geological repository.

Reprocessing Would Be Very Expensive

Reprocessing and the use of plutonium as reactor fuel are also far more expensive than using uranium fuel and disposing of the spent fuel directly. In the United States, some 60,000 tons of nuclear waste have already been produced, and existing reactors add some 2,000 metric tons of spent fuel annually. The Energy Department recently released an industry estimate that a reprocessing plant with an annual capacity of 2,000 metric tons of spent fuel would cost up to $20 billion to build—and the US would need two of these to reprocess all its spent fuel. An Argonne National Laboratory scientist recently estimated that the cost premium for reprocessing spent fuel would range from 0.4 to 0.6 cents per kilowatt-hour—corresponding to an extra $3 to $4.5 billion per year for the current US nuclear reactor fleet. The American public would end up having to pay this charge, either through increased taxes or higher electricity bills.

Building Nuclear Plants Takes Years and Is Expensive

Jim Green

Jim Green is editor of the Nuclear Monitor, *a magazine for the global anti-nuclear community.*

Nuclear Power Is Not a Silver Bullet

> *"Saying that nuclear power can solve global warming by itself is way over the top".*
>
> — *Senior International Atomic Energy Agency energy analyst Alan McDonald, 2004.*

N uclear power could at most make a modest contribution to climate change abatement. The main limitation is that it is used almost exclusively for electricity generation, which accounts for less than 25% of global (anthropogenic) greenhouse emissions.

Doubling current nuclear capacity would reduce emissions by roughly 6% if nuclear displaced coal—or not at all if nuclear displaced renewables and energy efficiency. Doubling nuclear power generation would require building 437 reactors to add to the 437 existing 'operable' reactors (380 gigawatts). It would also require new reactors to replace shut-down reactors—the International Energy Agency anticipates almost 200 shut downs by 2040.

A 2007 report by the International Panel on Fissile Materials (IPFM) states that if nuclear power grew approximately three-fold to about 1000 GWe in 2050, the increase in global greenhouse emissions projected in business-as-usual scenarios could be reduced by about 10–20%—assuming that nuclear displaced coal. The IPFM scenario (which it does not advocate) assumes a

"Nuclear Power: No Solution to Climate Change," by Jim Green, Wise International, June 25, 2016. Reprinted by permission.

business-as-usual doubling of greenhouse emissions by 2050, with 700 additional reactors reducing emissions from 14 billion metric tons to 13 billion metric tons. Thus the *increase* in emissions would be reduced by 1/7 or 14% and *overall* emissions would be reduced by 1/14 or 7%—assuming that nuclear displaces coal.

According to a 2007 article in *Progress in Nuclear Energy*, a ten-fold increase in nuclear capacity by the end of the century would reduce greenhouse emissions by 15%.

Clearly, nuclear power is not a 'silver bullet'.

Greenhouse Emissions from the Nuclear Fuel Cycle

Claims that nuclear power is 'greenhouse free' are false. Nuclear power is more greenhouse intensive than most renewable energy sources and energy efficiency measures. Life-cycle greenhouse emissions from nuclear power will increase as relatively high-grade uranium ores are mined out and give way to the mining of lower-grade ores.

Greenhouse emissions arise across the nuclear fuel cycle—uranium mining, milling, conversion, and enrichment; reactor construction, refurbishment and decommissioning; waste management (e.g. reprocessing, and/or encasement in glass or cement); and transportation of uranium, spent fuel, etc.

[...]

Life-cycle greenhouse emissions from nuclear power will increase as relatively high-grade uranium ores are mined out. In 2009, mining consultancy firm CRU Group calculated that the average grade of uranium projects at the feasibility study stage around the world was 35% lower than the grades of operating mines, and that exploration projects had average grades 60% below existing operations.

The extent of the increase in the greenhouse intensity of uranium mining is the subject of debate and considerable uncertainty. It depends not only on declining ore grades but also on other variables such as the choice of tailings management options at uranium mines.

Writing in the *Journal of Industrial Ecology* in 2012, Warner and Heath stated that emissions from the nuclear fuel cycle could increase by 55–220% with declining uranium ore grades.

Academic Dr Mark Diesendorf states: "In the case where high-grade uranium ore is used, CO_2 emissions from the nuclear fuel cycle are much less than those of an equivalent gas-fired power station. But the world's reserves of high-grade uranium are very limited and may only last a few decades. The vast majority of the world's uranium is low-grade. CO_2 emissions from mining, milling and enrichment of low-grade uranium are substantial, and so total CO_2 emissions from the nuclear fuel cycle become greater than or equal to those of a gas-fired power station."

Keith Barnham, Emeritus Professor of Physics at Imperial College London, states that for ore with uranium concentration around 0.01%, the carbon footprint of nuclear electricity could be as high as that of electricity generation from natural gas.

The German Environment Ministry stated in a 2006 report that a modern gas-fired power station in connection with heat production (co-generation) could be less carbon intensive than nuclear power.

Some nuclear lobbyists claim that Generation IV fast neutron reactors would reduce emissions from the nuclear fuel cycle by using waste products (esp. depleted uranium and spent fuel) as fuel instead of mined uranium. One of the problems with that arguments is that Generation IV reactors are—and always have been—decades away.

[...]

As for the real-world experience with fast neutron reactors, for the most part they have failed every test including carbon intensity. White elephants such as Japan's Monju reactor and France's Superphenix produced so little electricity that the carbon intensity must have been high. Monju operated for 205 days after it was connected to the grid in August 1995, and a further 45 days in 2010; apart from that it has been shut-down because of a sodium leak and fire in 1996, and a 2010 accident when a

3.3 tonne refuelling machine fell into the reactor vessel. The lifetime load factor of the French Superphenix fast reactor—the ratio of electricity generated compared to the amount that would have been generated if operated continually at full capacity—was just 7% percent, making it one of the worst-performing reactors in history.

Nuclear Power—A Slow Response to an Urgent Problem

Expanding nuclear power is impractical as a short-term response to the need to urgently reduce greenhouse emissions. The industry does not have the capacity to rapidly expand production as a result of 20 years of stagnation. Limitations include bottlenecks in the reactor manufacturing sector, dwindling and ageing workforces, and the considerable time it takes to build a reactor and to pay back the energy debt from construction.

One constraint is the considerable time it takes to build reactors. The World Nuclear Industry Status Report 2014 noted that the average construction time of the last 37 reactors that started up was 10 years; and that at least 49 of the 67 reactors listed as under construction have encountered construction delays.

The development of new reactor types—even those which are just modified versions of conventional reactor technology—further delays the construction and deployment of nuclear power. For example the EPR in Finland is 7–9 years behind schedule, and the EPR in France is five years behind schedule (and counting).

Nuclear power is still slower for countries building their first reactor. The IAEA sets out a phased 'milestone' approach to establishing nuclear power in new countries, lasting from 11–20 years: a pre-project phase 1 (1–3 years), a project decision-making phase (3–7 years) and a construction phase (7–10 years).

The French Nuclear Safety Authority (ASN) says that the initial development of a nuclear power industry requires at least 10–15 years in order to build up skills in safety and control and to develop a regulatory framework—that's 10–15 years even before reactor construction begins. Even with rapid progress, ASN estimates a minimum lead time of 15 years before a new nuclear power plant can be started up in a country that does not already have the required infrastructure.

In addition to reactor construction, further years elapse before nuclear power has generated as much as energy as was expended in the construction of the reactor. One academic report states: "The energy payback time of nuclear energy is around 6½ years for light water reactors, and 7 years for heavy water reactors, ranging within 5.6–14.1 years, and 6.4–12.4 years, respectively."

By contrast, construction times for renewable energy sources are typically months not years, and likewise the energy pay-back period is typically months not years.

[…]

Another constraint is the pattern of ageing nuclear workforces— the 'silver tsunami'. In the UK, for example, a recent government report says that attrition rates in the ageing nuclear workforce are "high and growing" with more than 8,000 new employees a year needed every year for the next six years if the country's ambitious new-build programme is to succeed. In addition, research and training facilities and courses have been on the decline.

A major expansion of nuclear power is theoretically possible over the medium- to long-term. The depletion of uranium resources could be a constraint. According to the World Nuclear Association, the world's present measured resources of uranium (5.9 Mt) in the cost category around 1.5 times present spot prices, are enough to last for about 90 years at the current usage rate of 66,000 tU/yr.

Nuclear Power and Climate Change

Countries and regions with a high reliance on nuclear power also tend to have high greenhouse gas emissions. For example, the US operates 99 power reactors with a capacity of 98.8 GW (26% of the world total), with nuclear power generating over 19% of its electricity. Yet the US is one of the world's largest greenhouse polluters both in *per capita* and overall terms.

Some countries are planning to replace fossil fuel-fired power plants with nuclear power in order to increase fossil fuel exports. In such cases any potential climate change mitigation benefits of nuclear power are lost. World Nuclear News reported in 2010 that Venezuela, Russia, and some Middle East countries such as the UAE and Iran would prefer to export oil and gas rather than use them in domestic power plants.[30] Saudi Arabia is another country planning to build nuclear power plants in order to boost fossil fuel exports.

Climate Change and Nuclear Hazards

Nuclear power plants are vulnerable to threats which are being exacerbated by climate change—discussed in detail in Nuclear Monitor #770.

A 2013 report by the US Department of Energy details many of the interconnections between climate change and energy. These include:

- Increasing risk of shutdowns at thermoelectric power plants (e.g. coal, gas and nuclear) due to decreased water availability which affects cooling, a requirement for operation;
- Higher risks to energy infrastructure located along the coasts due to sea level rise, the increasing intensity of storms, and higher storm surge and flooding;
- Disruption of fuel supplies during severe storms;
- Power plant disruptions due to drought; and
- Power lines, transformers and electricity distribution systems face increasing risks of physical damage from the hurricanes, storms and wildfires that are growing more frequent and intense.

At the lower end of the risk spectrum, there are many instances of nuclear plants operating at reduced power or being temporarily shut down due to water shortages or increased water temperature (which can adversely affect reactor cooling and/or cause fish deaths and other problems with the dumping of waste heat in water sources). Reactors in several countries have been forced to close during heat waves, when they're needed the most. For example, France had to purchase power from the UK in 2009 because almost a third of its nuclear generating capacity was lost when it had to cut production to avoid exceeding thermal discharge limits.

At the upper end of the risk spectrum, climate-related threats pose serious risks, such as storms cutting off grid power, leaving nuclear plants reliant on generators for reactor cooling. A 2004 incident in Germany illustrates the risks. Both Biblis reactors (A and B) were in operation when heavy storms knocked out power lines. Because of an incorrectly set electrical switch and a faulty pressure gauge, the Biblis-B turbine did not drop, as designed, from 1,300 to 60 megawatts. Instead the reactor scrammed. When Biblis-B scrammed with its grid power supply already cut off, four emergency diesel generators started. Another emergency supply also started but, because of a switching failure, one of the lines failed to connect. These lines would have been relied upon as a backup to bring emergency power from Biblis-B to Biblis-A if Biblis-A had also been without power. The result was a partial disabling of the emergency power supply from Biblis-B to Biblis-A for about two hours.

"Water wars" will become increasingly common with climate change—in particular, disputes over the allocation of increasingly scarce water resources between power generation and agriculture. Nuclear power reactors consume massive amounts of water—typically 36.3 to 65.4 million litres per reactor per day—primarily for reactor cooling.

[...]

Weapons Proliferation and Nuclear Winter

Global expansion of nuclear power would inevitably involve the growth and spread of stockpiles of weapons-useable fissile material and the facilities to produce fissile materials (enrichment plants for highly enriched uranium; and reactors and reprocessing plants for plutonium). Global expansion of nuclear power would lead to an increase in the number of "threshold" or "breakout" nuclear states which could quickly produce weapons drawing on expertise, facilities and materials from their "civil" nuclear program.

Former US Vice President Al Gore has neatly summed up the problem: "For eight years in the White House, every weapons-proliferation problem we dealt with was connected to a civilian reactor program. And if we ever got to the point where we wanted to use nuclear reactors to back out a lot of coal ... then we'd have to put them in so many places we'd run that proliferation risk right off the reasonability scale."

Running the proliferation risk off the reasonability scale brings the debate back to climate change—a connection explained by Alan Robock in *The Bulletin of the Atomic Scientists*:

> *As recent work ... has shown, we now understand that the atmospheric effects of a nuclear war would last for at least a decade – more than proving the nuclear winter theory of the 1980s correct. By our calculations, a regional nuclear war between India and Pakistan using less than 0.3% of the current global arsenal would produce climate change unprecedented in recorded human history and global ozone depletion equal in size to the current hole in the ozone, only spread out globally.*

Nuclear expansion would also increase the availability of nuclear materials for radioactive 'dirty bombs'. It would also increase the number of potential targets for terrorist attacks or conventional military strikes by nation-states (such as the repeated military strikes and attempted strikes on nuclear sites in the Middle East).

The US National Intelligence Council argued in a 2008 report that the "spread of nuclear technologies and expertise is generating concerns about the potential emergence of new nuclear weapon states and the acquisition of nuclear materials by terrorist groups."

As long ago as 1946, the Acheson-Lilienthal Report commissioned by the US Department of State identified intractable problems:

> *We have concluded unanimously that there is no prospect of security against atomic warfare in a system of international*

agreements to outlaw such weapons controlled only by a system which relies on inspection and similar police-like methods. The reasons supporting this conclusion are not merely technical, but primarily the inseparable political, social, and organizational problems involved in enforcing agreements between nations each free to develop atomic energy but only pledged not to use it for bombs. National rivalries in the development of atomic energy readily convertible to destructive purposes are the heart of the difficulty.

Fissile Materials

A May 2015 report written by Zia Mian and Alexander Glaser for the International Panel on Fissile Materials provides details on stockpiles of fissile materials. As of the end of 2013, civilian stockpiles contained 57,070 weapon-equivalents: 61 tons of highly enriched uranium (4,070 weapons), and 267 tons of (separated) plutonium (53,000 weapons). The figures are far greater if plutonium in spent fuel is included.

Harold Feiveson calculates that with an increase in nuclear power capacity to 3,500 GW (compared to 380 GW as of June 2015), about 700 tonnes of plutonium would be produced annually. That amount of plutonium would suffice to build 70,000 nuclear weapons, and if we assume an average 40-year reactor lifespan the accumulated plutonium would suffice to build 2.8 million weapons.

Similarly, the Intergovernmental Panel on Climate Change maps out a scenario whereby nuclear capacity would grow to about 3,300 gigawatts in 2100 and the accumulated plutonium inventory would rise to 50-100 thousand tonnes (IPCC, 1995). That amount of plutonium would suffice to build 5–10 million nuclear weapons.

The challenge is still greater as a result of the practice of plutonium stockpiling. Japan's plutonium stockpiling, for example, clearly fans proliferation risks and tensions in north-east Asia. Diplomatic cables in 1993 and 1994 from US Ambassadors in Tokyo questioned the rationale for the stockpiling of so much plutonium. A 1993 US diplomatic cable posed these questions: "Can Japan expect that if it embarks on a massive plutonium recycling program that Korea and other nations would not press ahead with reprocessing programs? Would not the perception of Japan's being awash in plutonium and possessing leading edge rocket technology create anxiety in the region?"

A 2007 report by the International Panel on Fissile Materials (IPFM) states:

> Even a modest expansion of nuclear power would be accompanied by a substantial increase in the number of countries with nuclear reactors. Some of these countries would likely seek gas-centrifuge uranium-enrichment plants as well. Centrifuge-enrichment plants can be quickly converted to the production of highly enriched uranium for weapons. It is therefore critical to find multinational alternatives to the proliferation of national enrichment plants.
>
> If a large-scale expansion of nuclear power were accompanied by a shift to reprocessing and plutonium recycle in light-water or fast reactors, it would involve annual flows of separated plutonium on the scale of a thousand metric tons per year—enough for 100,000 nuclear bombs.

[...]

Nobody Wants Nuclear Energy

Ben Paulos

Ben Paulos is the principal of PaulosAnalysis, consulting and writing on clean energy policy, technology, and trend, for clients in the nonprofit, media, industry, and philanthropic sectors. He is currently directing the Power Markets Project, looking at the impact of renewable energy on electricity market designs in Germany and the US.

> *"We dance round in a ring and suppose, but the Secret sits in the middle and knows."*
>
> – Robert Frost

The US nuclear power industry is in trouble, with as many as 15 to 20 plants at risk of closure, according to the Nuclear Energy Institute. This has spurred a flurry of advocacy by nuclear plant owners, assisted by some advocates concerned about the impact on carbon emissions if they are replaced by fossil fuels.

But nuclear's long history has created a complicated landscape that makes easy answers hard to find.

For instance, nuclear power is cheap to operate, but wickedly expensive to build and repair. It is clean in terms of air pollution, but creates deadly radioactive waste. It is safe, unless there is an accident. It gets fewer direct federal subsidies than renewables, but has enjoyed decades of taxpayer funded research, job training, licensing, and finance, and would not exist without federally subsidized insurance.

Most ironically of all, it is strongly supported by free market conservatives, yet can only exist in a centrally planned economy where it is sheltered from any investment or market risk.

"The secret about nuclear power," by Ben Paulos, The Heinrich Boell Foundation, June 20, 2016. Reprinted by permission.

These contradictions have rich potential for creating confusion among citizens, the press, and elected officials.

But the people who actually make the decisions about our electric system are less confused. As far as banks, regulators and utility executives are concerned, nuclear power is radioactive.

Dancing in a Ring

There is a ring of advocacy around nuclear power, with groups like the Breakthrough Institute and Third Way, prominent climate scientist James Hansen, and '60s era environmentalist Stewart Brand helping the Nuclear Energy Institute and a few nuke-owning utilities. The advocates are driven by the idea that nuclear power is needed to reduce carbon emissions, since they think wind and solar are inadequate to the task. The industry is simply trying to extend the life of valuable assets in the face of competitive pressures.

For many years, the industry promoted a "nuclear renaissance" that would be ushered in by a new generation of advanced reactors—smaller and cheaper, with passive safety features—or by the generation after that, with exotic technologies like thorium. They were successful in winning supportive policies from Congress and some states, including R&D, loan guarantees, streamlined licensing, and a production tax credit (PTC), similar to one for wind power, worth about $850 million per year for new plants. Less touted but probably most important of all is "construction work in progress," or CWIP, where state regulators force customers to pay for a plant before it is finished, since banks won't make such a risky investment.

The problem with the renaissance was that few utilities were interested.

Two new projects are being built, but they use conventional technology, not advanced. In Georgia, the Southern Company is adding two more reactors to their Plant Vogtle. Original costs were estimated at $6.1 billion, but the project is three years behind schedule and 50 percent over budget. In South Carolina, the V.C. Summer plant is being built by South Carolina Electric & Gas and

Santee Cooper, a state-owned utility. That two-reactor plant was estimated at $9.8 billion, but costs have risen to at least $12 billion. Both projects rely on CWIP, federal loan guarantees, and federal tax credits.

The Watts Bar plant was recently finished by the Tennessee Valley Authority—but 44 years after construction began. The project was launched in 1972 and suspended in 1985, only to be revived in 2007.

Rear Guard Actions

With the nuclear renaissance foundering, advocates have retreated to a more pressing concern, helping utilities keep existing plants alive. Wholesale market prices have fallen in many regions of the US, due to greater energy efficiency, flat demand, cheap natural gas from fracking, and the rapid growth of wind and solar power. Nuclear plants in competitive markets, especially smaller ones with just one reactor, are struggling to compete.

In recent years, eight plants have been closed or slated for closing due to poor economics. Other plants, like San Onofre and Crystal River, have been closed in the face of massive repair bills.

To protect existing plants from the rigors of competition, the plan now for nuclear owners and proponents is to change the rules to bring in more revenues, or in their words, to "properly value the attributes" of nuclear power. One strategy proposed in New York and Illinois is to change state renewable energy mandates to "zero emission" mandates, making nuclear power eligible. New York is expected to issue a plan this summer while the Illinois legislature adjourned recently without taking action.

The Secret

Outside the few utilities that own nuclear plants, there is very little interest in nuclear. The people who actually make the decisions about the power system—regulators and utility executives—have moved on.

In a recent industry survey by Utility Dive, executives put nuclear power near the bottom of their list of concerns. Only

11 percent thought their utility should invest more in new nuclear generation, compared to 65 percent for storage and 47 percent for renewables.

Another survey by PWC found that globally, only 26 percent of utility executives thought nuclear power would have a "big impact" on their market by 2030, compared to 71 percent for energy efficient technologies and 60 percent for solar.

In a global trend toward competition in the utility sector, the financial risks of nuclear have made it the odd man out. Nuclear plants cost billions of dollars to build and repair and have lead times of ten years or more, making it impossible to predict what future revenues will be. If investors have to bear the risk of investment, rather than captive consumers, they won't touch nuclear.

Wind and solar power are modular and quick, meaning they can be developed in any size with lead times of less than a year. Global trade in technology means they can survive the ups and downs of any individual market. And heavy competition creates relentless pressure for improvement and cost reductions.

It's been clear for some time that new nuclear is not competitive. The surprise now is that even existing nuclear plants can't compete with gas, efficiency, and renewables.

While advocates argue that nuclear doesn't get as much policy support as renewables—a debatable point—the problems go much deeper. The secret is that nuclear power is not compatible with 21st century markets and policies. No amount of dancing will change that.

CHAPTER 4

Is Hydraulic Fracturing, or Fracking, Safe for Humans and the Environment?

Fracking Controversy and Communication

Hilary Boudet, Christopher Clarke, Dylan Bugden,
Edward Maibach, Connie Roser-Renouf, and
Anthony Leiserowitz

Boudet is an assistant professor in the department of sociology at
the School of Public Policy at Oregon State University. Bugden is an
affiliate of the School of Public Policy at Oregon State University.
Clarke, Maibach, and Roser-Renouf are affiliates of George Mason
University's department of communication. Leiserowitz is affiliated
with the Yale University School of Forestry and Environmental Studies.

The rapid development of unconventional sources of oil and natural gas using hydraulic fracturing has generated a great deal of controversy. Supporters have argued that fracking will spur economic growth, lead to more secure domestic energy supplies, and facilitate a rapid transition away from carbon-intensive, coal-based electricity generation (The Perryman Group, 2008; Considine et al., 2010; Hultman et al., 2011; US Environmental Protection Agency, 2011). Opponents have focused on potential adverse impacts to public health, the environment, and communities in close proximity to these energy sources (Colorado Department of Public Health and Environment, 2010; Osborn et al., 2011; Perry, 2012; Stedman et al., 2012). Given these conflicts, understanding public support and opposition is critical for planners tasked with addressing siting disputes and other issues (Boudet and Ortolano, 2010); for government agencies attempting to establish appropriate regulations (New York State Department of Environmental Conservation, 2013); and for researchers, advocates, and others interested in communicating about potential impacts (Clarke et al., in press). Using a nationally representative sample (N=1,061),

Reprinted from "'Fracking' controversy and communication: Using national survey data to understand public perceptions of hydraulic fracturing," by Hilary Boudet, Chris Clarke, Dylan Bugden, Edward Maibach, Connie Roser-Renouf and Anthony Leiserowitz, with permission from Elsevier.

we examine Americans' perceptions of hydraulic fracturing (i.e. "top of mind" associations); familiarity with the issue; levels of support/opposition; and predictors of such judgments. We draw on scholarship on public perceptions of emerging technology and discuss implications related to risk communication and energy policy.

What Is Hydraulic Fracturing?

Hydraulic fracturing ("fracking") is a technique for tapping unconventional oil and gas reserves that are otherwise inaccessible. In the early 2000s, energy companies began combining horizontal (or directional) drilling with hydraulic fracturing to tap these reserves (Armstrong et al., 1995). The process involves drilling horizontally through a rock layer and injecting a pressurized mixture of water, sand, and other chemicals that fractures the rock and facilitates the flow of oil and gas (Pye and Pye, 1973). These combined methods have allowed for expanded oil/gas development in shale and other formations in the US, Europe, Asia, Australia, and elsewhere (Clarke et al., in press; Walser and Pursell, 2007). The rapid expansion of fracking is projected to make the US a net exporter of natural gas in the coming years (David, 2013) and potentially the world's largest oil producer by 2017 (Mackey, 2012). Shale gas, which currently accounts for 23% of the nation's natural gas production, is projected to increase to 49% by 2035 (US Energy Information Administration, 2012).

Impacts Associated with Hydraulic Fracturing and Unconventional Oil/Gas Development

Hydraulic fracturing is just one part of the unconventional oil/gas development process, which also includes clearing land for well pads; construction of access roads and ancillary infrastructure (e.g., pipelines, compressor stations); transporting and processing fossil fuels extracted; transporting millions of gallons of water and wastewater for treatment/disposal; and bringing large (and often transient) populations to a community. These activities involve potential economic, environmental, social, and health impacts associated with rapid population growth in communities and boom-bust cycles of energy extraction (Jacquet, 2009). Both the extent and management of these impacts depend on numerous factors, including the development time frame (short- vs. long-term) and characteristics of the impacted area, such as population and the history of fossil fuel extraction (Brasier et al., 2011). We summarize some of the major issues that have emerged.

One of the biggest areas of contention involves the potential economic benefits of development, including job creation; increased income and wealth for individuals who sign gas leases on private lands; expanded local business opportunities for those who directly (i.e., construction) and indirectly service the energy industry (i.e., hotels and restaurants); and rising tax revenue for communities (Kay, 2011). For example, Theodori's (2009) key informants in two Texas counties with natural gas drilling in the Barnett Shale perceived increasing city revenues, property values, retail business, and household income; an expanding job market; and improving public services. Anderson's and Theodori's (2009) survey respondents from the same counties perceived a higher availability of good jobs. However, communities may face strains on public services such as schools, recreation facilities, water and sewage, and healthcare as well as infrastructure such as roads, all due to increased demand as new workers and industry move into an area (Jacquet, 2009). Anderson and Theodori's (2009) informants, for example, expressed concerns about increased truck traffic and damage to local roads as a result of nearby drilling.

A second major impact relates to water availability and quality. Hydraulic fracturing requires 2–10 million gallons of water per well per fracture (Soeder and Kappel, 2009), which raises concerns about depletion of surface or ground water sources. Also, contamination of subterranean and surface water can occur because of the release into rivers and streams of inadequately treated drilling wastewater with potentially toxic materials; surface spills of chemicals; and methane migration from gas wells into aquifers (Kargbo et al., 2010). Instances of water contamination allegedly tied to unconventional oil/gas drilling (Osborn et al., 2011) have prompted the EPA (2011) to examine the relationship between hydraulic fracturing and drinking water quality from an environmental and a public health perspective. Federal and state agencies have also issued regulations related to the disclosure of the chemical components of hydraulic fracturing fluid (Groeger, 2012). Such issues have influenced public perceptions of hydraulic fracturing. For example, Anderson's and Theodori's (2009) Texas informants listed water availability and groundwater depletion as concerns. Theodori's (2009) survey respondents stated that the "amount of freshwater used by gas producers," the "depletion of aquifers," and "water pollution" were all increasing.

Social impacts are a third area of focus, as they involve a community's ability to accommodate the frenzied activity associated with an energy development boom. Brasier et al. (2011) noted that social impacts include "[increased] stress, [changing] patterns of interactions within communities, [decreased] community cohesion, and [changing community] character" as new people move to a community to seek employment (p. 36). As a result, "individuals' quality of life, ties to community members, and mental and physical health [could] also be affected, leading to increases in social problems" (p. 36). For example, Theodori's (2009) respondents believed that "crime," "respect for law and order," and "disagreements among local residents" were becoming worse due to natural gas drilling. However, evidence suggests that, over time, communities can adapt to at least some of these changes (Brown et al., 2005).

Opinion Polling Data on Public Perceptions of Hydraulic Fracturing

Numerous national and state-level public opinion polls have focused on public perception of unconventional oil/gas development using hydraulic fracturing. National polling data points to somewhat strong public support for hydraulic fracturing, but with a sizable minority unsure or lacking familiarity with the issue. For example, a

Pew Research Center (2012) poll found that only 26% of Americans had heard a lot about the issue, 37% had heard a little, and 37% had heard nothing at all. Among those who had heard of it, 52% favored its use, and 35% were opposed. Similarly, the National Energy Opinion Poll (Vedlitz, 2012) found that only 21% of respondents reported "significant knowledge" about hydraulic fracturing, and a nonrepresentative 2012 University of Texas Energy Poll (2013) found that just 32% of respondents were familiar with it.

Opinion polling in states with active and/or proposed unconventional oil/gas development suggests more familiarity with hydraulic fracturing than at the national level. A 2011 survey of Pennsylvania residents found that 48% followed natural gas drilling in the Marcellus Shale "somewhat" or "very" closely. Forty-one percent felt that it was generating more benefits than problems; 33% said the problems were exceeding the benefits; and 26% said that benefits and problems were emerging in equal proportions. For perceptions of future benefits and problems, the figures were 50% expecting more benefits than problems, 32% more problems than benefits, and 17% about equal (Rabe and Borick, 2011). Similarly, a Quinnipiac University (2012a) poll found that 64% of Ohio residents believed that the economic benefits of hydraulic fracturing outweighed the environmental risks, and 85% believed it would bring jobs to the state. In New York, where the process is on hold pending environmental review, residents were more divided. Forty-four percent of New Yorkers were opposed and 43% in favor. Also, 45% believed that the economic benefits would outweigh environmental concerns; 81% felt drilling would create jobs; and 48% thought it would damage the environment (Quinnipiac University, 2012b).

[…]

Domestic and Cheap, Natural Gas Makes Sense

The Institute for Energy Research

The Institute for Energy Research (IER) is a not-for-profit organization that conducts intensive research and analysis on the functions, operations, and government regulation of global energy markets.

Less than a decade ago, natural gas prices in the United States were among the highest in the world. However, in the last five years, domestic natural gas reserves have grown 30 percent due to technological advances in the use of hydraulic fracturing, a drilling method that is coupled with directional drilling to access underground reservoirs of oil and gas. This technological breakthrough had an immediate impact on natural gas prices, causing them to plummet and remain low to the present time.

Despite this important stride toward future US energy security, hydraulic fracturing has come under attack. As the newest *cause célèbre* of fossil fuel foes, hydraulic fracturing was notably featured in the 2010 movie *Gasland,* which dramatized the allegation that hydraulic fracturing had been the cause of groundwater contamination. Understandably, these reports have caused much public consternation, and have prompted both regulators and legislators to contemplate whether hydraulic fracturing should be subject to additional federal regulation. But are they accurate?

What Is Hydraulic Fracturing?

While the controversy over hydraulic fracturing is new, hydraulic fracturing itself is not. First used in 1947, hydraulic fracturing has been employed in more than a million wells to extract more than 7 billion barrels of oil and 600 trillion feet of natural gas from deep

"Hydraulic Fracturing—Is It Safe?" The Institute for Energy Research. The Institute for Energy Research is a 501(c)(3) public foundation that conducts research on the functions, operations and government regulation of global energy markets, May 3, 2011. Reprinted by permission.

underground shale formations. Geologists have long known that shale rock formations contain large amounts of natural gas and oil, but the fossil fuel resources were trapped in layers of rock and could not easily be extracted.

During the initial phase of the fracturing operation, a well is drilled vertically underground to a point past the deepest aquifer containing fresh groundwater. At this stage, the operator inserts steel surface casing down the length of the drilled hole, then pumps in cement to create a barrier of cement and steel between the groundwater and the well bore. The well is then drilled further down into the underground shale formation, where the operator detonates charges in order to create spaces in rock pores to release oil and gas. To create additional fissures, fracturing fluids are injected into the formation at high pressure, which contain additives such as sand to keep the fissures open and the hydrocarbons flowing.

Additionally, horizontal drilling provides more exposure within a formation than a vertical well—six to eight horizontal wells drilled from only one well pad can produce the same volume as sixteen vertical wells. This use of multi-well pads significantly reduces the overall infrastructure needed for an operation, such as access roads, pipelines routes, and production facilities, thereby minimizing disturbances to the habitat and impacts to the public.

Is It Safe for Groundwater Resources?

Two studies conducted by the Environmental Protection Agency (EPA) and the Ground Water Protection Council (GWPC)—the national association of state ground water and underground injection agencies whose mission is to promote the protection and conservation of ground water—found that there have been no confirmed incidents of groundwater contamination from hydraulic fracturing. This is particularly noteworthy in consideration of the fact that approximately one million wells have been hydraulically fractured in the United States. Furthermore, according to the Interstate Oil and Gas Compact Commission (IOGCC)—the multi-state governmental agency representing states' oil and gas interests—each IOGCC member state has confirmed that there has not been a case of groundwater contamination where hydraulic fracturing was attributed to be the cause.

Despite this, much ado has been made regarding the use of hydraulic fracturing fluids and their potential to contaminate groundwater. Fracturing fluids consist predominately of water and sand—98 percent or more in a typical fracturing solution—while the rest is made up of high-viscosity chemical additives designed to maximize the effectiveness of the fracture job. Many of the additives consist of common household compounds, and while you certainly wouldn't want to go out of your way to drink them, the EPA concluded in a 2004 study that the additives are not considered harmful to human life or the environment in the capacity they are used. Additionally, the formula for each fracturing fluid used in a drilling operation must, by mandate of the Occupational Safety and Health Administration, be disclosed at each drilling site, and a coalition of state groundwater and oil and gas regulators recently launched the Frac Focus Chemical Disclosure Registry to allow companies to voluntarily disclose the content of fracturing fluids used at individual well sites. Within 10 days of the site's launch, 32 companies disclosed chemicals used at 388 wells.

Furthermore, stringent state and federal regulations on well design and construction ensure that fracturing fluid additives do not migrate upward into active or treatable water reservoirs. As aforementioned, groundwater is protected during the process of hydraulic fracturing by steel and cement casing that is installed when the well is first drilled to isolate groundwater resources. Operators have a further interest in ensuring that fractures are sufficiently well removed from underground water resources, as the penetration of a water table above a formation could render the oil and gas resources unusable.

After a fracturing job has been completed, the majority of fracturing fluids are recovered from the well and recycled in a closed system for future use. Surface disposals of fracturing fluid are subject to the federal Clean Water Act, requiring treatment for any potentially harmful substances prior to discharge, or the federal Safe Drinking Water Act if disposed in an oil and gas injection well.

How Much Shale Gas Do We Have?

The US has an abundant amount of natural gas. The Energy Information Administration estimates that the US has in excess of 2,119 trillion cubic feet (Tcf) of technically recoverable natural gas, enough to power the US for 88 years at current rates of consumption. Unconventional resources, like shale gas, account for 60 percent of the onshore recoverable resources, representing an enormous advancement in the United States' future energy outlook. In fact, half of the gas consumed today was produced from wells drilled within the last 3.5 years.

Most of the natural gas consumed in the United States is produced domestically—approximately 89 percent in 2010—and much of this supply comes from Texas, Wyoming, and Oklahoma. However, shale gas is present in many of the lower 48 states, in shale plays or basins.

The economic impact of this vast resource cannot be understated. In 2008, after breakthroughs in hydraulic fracturing yielded access to unconventional gas deposits, the wellhead price of natural gas plummeted from nearly $8 per thousand cubic feet to $3.67 per thousand cubic feet. In 2009, the United States was the world's largest natural gas producer, and of the 24.1 Tcf of natural gas that Americans consumed in 2010, just 2.6 Tcf, or 11 percent, was provided from net imports.

In addition to keeping prices low for American consumers—who get 24 percent of their electricity from natural gas—increased domestic production also creates jobs and generates royalties for residents, cities, and school districts. For example, a recent study estimates that in 2009, the development of the Marcellus Shale created 44,000 new jobs in Pennsylvania, and added $389 million in state and local revenue, over $1 billion in federal tax revenue, and almost $4 billion in value added to the state's economy.

Who Should Regulate?

In its study "*State Oil and Gas Regulations Designed to Protect Water Resources,*" the GWPC found that all oil and gas producing states currently have regulations in place to provide protection for water resources during oil and gas exploration and production. Enacting national regulations for these activities would not only be duplicative and costly for states to implement, it would indicate a fundamental disregard for states' expertise in managing their own natural resources. Common sense dictates that states, with field operations, are in a better position to evaluate the hazards of a drilling operation than federal agencies whose operations are removed from the circumstance.

This is not to say that no federal regulations apply to hydraulic fracturing. Operations are subject to a number of federal statutes, including the Clean Water Act, Safe Drinking Water Act, the National Environmental Policy Act, and the Emergency Planning and Community Right-to-Know Act.

Conclusion

Recent attempts to portray hydraulic fracturing as a dangerous, unregulated practice are misleading at best. When done within the set parameters of the numerous state and federal regulations that govern safe drilling practices, hydraulic fracturing has the potential to provide the United States with an abundant supply of clean-burning natural gas for years to come. Rather than trying to reinvent the wheel with new federal mandates, regulators should defer to states who can tailor and apply regulations to suit their specific circumstances.

Policy decisions on hydraulic fracturing will have significant ramifications for our future energy security. According to the National Petroleum Council, up to 80 percent of natural gas wells drilled in the next decade will require hydraulic fracturing; one can only imagine the bureaucratic nightmare that would ensue upon granting the federal government with even more oversight of each operation. Indeed, the notion that the federal government would need to regulate on a well-to-well basis seems all the more incredible when juxtaposed with the industry's excellent safety record. As aforementioned, there has not been a single confirmed incident of groundwater contamination arising from hydraulic fracturing since the practice began in 1947.

Instead of bringing an already well-regulated practice under the yoke of the EPA, the federal government should refocus its efforts upon maintaining access to affordable, domestically produced energy. In a time of rising gasoline and food prices, American families cannot shoulder a hit on another essential commodity— nor should they be expected to.

Natural Gas Is a Clean Transition Fuel

Fang-Yu Liang, Marta Ryvak, Sara Sayeed, and Nick Zhao

Fang-Yu Liang is a research analyst at Environmental Financial Products and a teaching assistant at the University of Chicago Law School. Marta Ryvak, Sara Sayeed, and Nick Zhao conducted research at the University of Chicago.

Natural gas is formed in the earth's crust as a result of transformation of organic matter due to heat and pressure of overlying rock. The gas hydrocarbons can also be produced as a result of microbial decomposition of organic substances and due to reduction of mineral salts. Some of these gases are released into the atmosphere or hydrosphere while the rest accumulates in the upper layers of the earth's crust.

The composition of natural gas varies depending on a number of factors like the origin, location of deposit and geological structure. Natural gas mainly consists of saturated aliphatic hydrocarbons like methane. Components such as carbon dioxide, hydrogen sulfide, nitrogen and helium constitute an insignificant proportion of natural gas composition. Natural gas is the cleanest of all fossil fuels and the main products of combustion of natural gas are carbon dioxide and water vapor. The combustion of natural gas releases very small amounts of nitrogen oxides (NO_x), sulfur dioxide (SO_2), carbon dioxide (CO_2), carbon monoxide (CO), other reactive hydrocarbons and virtually no particulate matter. Coal and oil are composed of much more complex molecules and when combusted, they release higher levels of harmful emissions such as nitrogen oxides and sulfur dioxide. They also release ash particles into the environment.

"The role of natural gas as a primary fuel in the near future, including comparisons of acquisition, transmission and waste handling costs of as with competitive alternatives," Fang-Yu Liang, Marta Ryvak, Sara Sayeed and Nick Zhao, Liang et al.; licensee BioMed Central Ltd, April 23, 2012. https://ccj.springeropen.com/articles/10.1186/1752-153X-6-S1-S4. Licensed under CC BY 2.0

Natural gas can be used in many ways to help reduce the emissions of pollutants into the atmosphere as it emits fewer harmful pollutants and an increased reliance on natural gas can potentially reduce the emission of many of these harmful pollutants. In the United States the pollutants emitted from the combustion of fossil fuels have led to the development of a number of pressing environmental problems that include, but is not limited to:

- Emission of greenhouse gases, which could contribute to global warming
- Smog, air quality and acid rain, which is detrimental to human health and the wider ecosystem

Global warming is an environmental issue that deals with the potential for global climate changes due to the increased levels of atmospheric greenhouse gases. Scientists claim that an increase in greenhouse gases will lead to increased temperature around the globe. The principle greenhouse gases include carbon dioxide, water vapor, methane and nitrogen oxides. The levels of greenhouse gases in the atmosphere have been increasing due to the widespread burning of fossil fuels by the growing human populations.

The main component of natural gas, methane, is itself a potent greenhouse gas. Methane emissions account for only 1.1% of the total US greenhouse gas emissions, they account for 8.5% of the greenhouse gas emissions based on global warming potential. A study performed by the EPA (Environment Protection Agency) and the GRI (Gas Research Institute) in 1997 lead to the conclusion that the reduction of emissions from increased natural gas use would strongly outweigh the detrimental effects of increased methane emissions. Therefore the increased use of natural gas can serve to reduce the emission of greenhouse gases in the United States.

Smog is formed by a chemical reaction of carbon monoxide, nitrogen oxides, volatile organic compounds and heat from sunlight. Ground level ozone and smog can contribute to respiratory problems that range from temporary discomfort to permanent lung damage. The use of natural gas does not contribute to the formation of smog as it emits low levels of nitrogen oxides and no particulate matter. Increased natural gas use could be served to combat smog production. This would reduce the emissions of smog causing chemicals and result in healthier air.

Acid rain is formed when sulfur dioxide and nitrogen oxides react with water vapor and other chemical in the presence of sunlight. The increased use of natural gas could provide for fewer acid rain causing emissions.

Natural gas powered industrial application and natural gas fired electric generation offer a variety of environmental benefits and environmentally friendly uses that include:

1. Fewer GHG emissions
2. Re-burning: Natural gas can be added to coal or oil fired boilers to reduce NO_x and SO_2 emissions.
3. Reduced sludge: Sludge refers to the residual material left from industrial waste water, or sewage treatment processes. Coal-fired power plants and industrial boilers that use scrubbers to reduce SO_2 emission levels usually generate thousands of tons of harmful sludge. Natural gas releases insignificant amounts of SO_2, which eliminates the need for scrubbers, and thus reducing the amount of sludge from industrial processes.
4. Cogenerations: Cogeneration is the use of a heat engine or a power station to simultaneously generate both electricity and useful heat. The preferred fuel for new cogeneration equipment is natural gas.
5. Fuel cells
6. Combined cycle generation

Use of Natural Gas

Natural gas has a number of applications commercially in homes, industries and the transportation sector.

Industrial Uses

Natural gas helps provide base ingredients for products like plastic, fertilizer, anti-freeze and fabrics. Industry accounts for about 25% of natural gas use across all sectors. It is the second most used energy source in industry after electricity.

Natural gas is used primarily in the metal, chemical, petroleum refining, stone, clay and glass, pulp and paper, plastic and food-processing industries. These businesses account for more than 84% of the total industrial natural gas use. Natural gas is used for waste treatment and incineration, metal preheating, glass melting, drying and dehumidification, food processing and fueling industrial boilers. It is also used as feedstock for the manufacturing of a number of chemicals and products and as a building block for methanol, which has a number of industrial applications. Natural gas is converted to synthesis gas (a mixture of hydrogen and carbon oxides formed by the process of steam reforming. In the process, natural gas is exposed to a catalyst that causes oxidization of natural gas when brought in contact with steam). Synthesis gas is used to make methanol (can be used as fuel source in fuel cell)—used to make substances like formaldehyde, an additive for cleaner burning gasoline called MTBE (methyl tertiary butyl ether,) and acetic acid. Gases like butane, propane and ethane can be extracted from natural gas and these may be used as feedstock for products like fertilizers and pharmaceutical products.

Natural gas desiccant systems (used for dehumidification) are used in pharmaceutical, plastic, candy and recycling industries. The absorption systems used to heat and cool water in an economical, efficient and environmentally sound way.

Natural Gas in the Transportation Sector

According to natural gas vehicle coalition estimates there are 120,000 Natural Gas Vehicles (NGV) in USA and more than 8.7 million NGV worldwide. There are about 1,100 natural gas fueling stations in USA alone.

Disadvantages of NGV like limited range, trunk space, higher initial cost, lack of refueling infrastructure are impediments to future spread of NGV. Some natural gas vehicles are bi-fuel, so there is flexibility of fuel choice. Many of these vehicles were originally just gasoline but have been converted to be bi-fuel. Conversion is costly and results in less efficient use of natural gas.

Furthermore, natural gas use reduces environmentally harmful emissions associated with automobiles. Vehicles on the road account for 60% of the carbon monoxide pollution, 31% of the nitrogen oxides and 29% of the hydrocarbon emissions in USA. These emissions contribute to smog pollution and increase dangerous ground level ozone. Vehicles account for over half of all dangerous air pollutants and about 30% of the total carbon emissions in the USA. This contributes to the presence of greenhouse gases in the atmosphere. The environmental effects of NGV are less detrimental than that of others.

Due to the chemical composition of natural gas, NGV are much cleaner burning than others. Natural gas—methane mainly— emits small amounts of ethane, propane and butane. Gasoline/ diesel fuels—contain harmful compounds—emit sulfur dioxide and nitrogen oxides (combine in atmosphere to produce ground level ozone), arsenic, benzene, nickel and over 40 other toxic substances. NGV produce, on average, 70% less carbon monoxide, 80% less nitrogen oxides and 87% less nonmethane organic gas than other vehicles.

Supply in the US Market

The United States has the biggest gas market in world. Proven gas reserves amounted to 7.8 Tcm at the beginning of 2002, which is 4% of world gas reserves.

Due to new drilling technologies, such as hydraulic fracturing technology and horizontal drilling, that are unlocking substantial amounts of natural gas from shale rocks, the estimated gas reserves of the US have surged by 35% in 2009. Shale gas is trapped underground in bubbles between thin layers of shale rock. The report by the Potential Gas Committee, the authority on gas supplies, shows the United States holds far larger reserves than previously thought. In fact, leading industry experts now believe that North America has more than 3,000 trillion cubic feet of proved natural gas reserves—enough to meet the current rate of US consumption for more than 100 years. This finding raises the possibility that natural gas could emerge as a critical "transition fuel" that could be used to mitigate the cost of shifting into a clean energy economy.

The single largest source of US Natural Gas Supply is unconventional production, in particular natural gas in tight sand formations, which is predicted to accounts for 30% of total US production by 2030. Production from shale formations however, is the fastest growing source.

Summary and Conclusions

Given our research, we believe that there are several reasons for the United States to enhance the competitiveness of natural gas:

- Natural gas is a versatile fuel that can be used to power its residential heating, industrial, electrical generation, and transportation sectors for decades into the future.
- According to Seeking Alpha, The US uses 25% of the worldwide oil supply and imports 65% of it. Natural gas is the only US domestic fuel, besides from coal, that is abundant enough to reduce oil consumption over the next decade. The use of the vast US natural gas reserves and the nation's 2.2 million mile natural gas pipeline grid are the best way to reduce foreign oil imports.
- Natural gas is environmentally friendly and is the cleanest (closest to being carbon neutral), and in most cases the most economically viable "transition fuel" to a "Clean Tech" economy. For example, NVG emit 20% less CO_2 than gasoline powered internal combustion engines and no toxic particulates.
- Natural gas electrical generation is the preferred backup power supply for unreliable wind and solar energy. It is the ideal bridge to a renewable energy future.

- Natural gas electrical generators are more efficient and emit 50% less CO_2 than the coal-fired plants. They do not emit any of the particulate matter or ash.
- The natural gas infrastructure can be used by the future hydrogen energy based economy.
- The "impending doom" of global warming has heightened legislative efforts for a comprehensive national climate change policy. Despite the inertia in congress to pass a national legislation addressing climate change, the proliferation of regional voluntary programs/ efforts such as the RGGI, Californian AB '32, Chicago Climate Exchange, combined with competitive pressure on the international level (the success of the European Union Emissions Trading Scheme for example), will create an impetus for change. Investing in natural gas, therefore, is a strategic move.

[...]

When Done Right, Fracking Is Safe

Jacquelyn Pless

Jacquelyn Pless is an economist who studies topics in innovation, energy and environmental economics, public economics, and economic development.

I n recent years, technological advances in hydraulic fracturing and horizontal drilling have led to dramatic growth in natural gas development, with tremendous economic potential for state and local economies. Development currently is occurring in 32 states. Although hydraulic fracturing has been employed for decades, its use has rapidly increased in the past few years, and some states are taking steps to ensure that water and air quality are adequately protected during surface and subsurface natural gas development activities.

[...]

Public Health and the Environment

Although fracking to develop natural gas offers many benefits to state and local economies, its rapid expansion near densely populated areas has increased attention to its effects on human health and the environment. Cases of water contamination have been linked to natural gas operations, including incidences of spills and leaks. Recent research released by the Energy Institute at the University of Texas did not find a direct link between hydraulic fracturing and groundwater pollution problems. Rather, above-ground spills, leaking drill casings and wastewater mishandling can be sources of groundwater pollution.

Protecting Surface Water and Disposing of Wastewater

One growing concern is contamination of public drinking water. Fracking fluid could contain hazardous chemicals and, if mismanaged, spills could leak harmful substances into groundwater or surface water.

Since hydraulic fracturing produces wastewater that needs to be treated, states may consider regulatory oversight of wastewater storage and disposal.

Water Withdrawals

A deep shale gas well hydraulic fracturing operation can require 3 million to 5 million gallons of water. Although this is a significant amount of water, generating electricity with natural gas is less water-intensive compared to other forms of fossil fuel electricity generation.

Significant water withdrawal could affect aquatic habitats or water availability, particularly in regions where water supply is threatened. Innovative water use approaches are being pursued by industry. For example, recent research revealed that use of coal mine drainage is technically viable, although its economic viability may depend upon site-specific conditions.

Air Quality

Natural gas is efficient and clean compared to other fossil fuels, emitting 80 percent fewer nitrogen oxides, less sulfur dioxide, no mercury and very few particulates. Nonetheless, some remain concerned about air quality and greenhouse gas emissions. The drilling process potentially could release chemicals such as benzene and methane. According to the US Environmental Protection Agency (EPA), natural gas systems remain one of the most significant methane emitters in the United States, although the issue is being revisited due to lack of data.

The EPA recently finalized New Source Performance Standards for natural gas hydraulic fracturing operations to help reduce smog-forming air pollution and harmful air toxins. The new rules—

effective in 2015—are projected to reduce methane emissions and to reduce volatile organic compound emissions by 95 percent.

Surrounding Habitat

Increased exploration and development also affect surrounding habitat and wildlife. Vegetation and soils may be disturbed if gas wells require new roads, clearing and leveling. At the same time, advanced technologies in horizontal drilling and hydraulic fracturing allow energy companies to access far more natural gas from fewer wells.

Seismic Activity

Recent seismic activity in Ohio and Oklahoma is drawing attention to a possible link between earthquakes and deep wells used to dispose of hydraulic fracturing wastes. For instance, the Oklahoma Geological Survey is examining the possibility of induced seismicity from hydraulic fracturing. Pending S.B. 6903 in New York would require a seismological impact study related to hydraulic fracturing.

[...]

Water Quality Protection

State legislatures are taking a number of steps to help protect water quality by creating well location, water withdrawal, flowback or waste regulations, or setting casing and mechanical integrity requirements.

Spills and Leak Prevention Through Mechanical Integrity Tests or Casing Requirements

Recent research released by the Energy Institute at the University of Texas did not find a direct link between hydraulic fracturing and groundwater pollution problems. Rather, above-ground spills, leaking drill casings and wastewater mishandling may be more common causes of groundwater pollution. Possible solutions could include more stringent regulation of drill casings or other mechanical integrity measures to prevent spills or leaks.

Pending H.B. 3897 in Illinois, for example, would require integrity tests of casings or other mechanical testing prior to hydraulic fracturing. New York's pending A.B. 6540 would require certificates of competence to use a derrick or other drilling equipment, and a few pending bills in Pennsylvania (S.B. 425, H.B. 971 and H.B. 1645) address casing requirements.

Wastewater Transportation Requirements

Concern exists about possible spills during waste transportation after a hydraulic fracturing treatment, and some states are taking steps to help mitigate associated risks. Pennsylvania's pending H.B. 1741, for example, would require vehicles to display a placard on the outside of the vehicle indicating it is carrying hydraulic fracturing wastewater.

Regulations for Treating and Disposing Waste

States are addressing waste treatment and disposal in a variety of ways, partially due to unique geological factors, and some states are working to address these issues through legislation. Illinois' pending H.B. 3897, for example, addresses disposal and reuse of well stimulation fluid that is recovered during flowback, and S.B. 3280 addresses storage of such fluids. Two pending bills in New Jersey (A.B. 575 and S.B. 253) would prohibit treatment, discharge, disposal or storage of fracking operations wastewater in the state.

In New York, A.B. 6488 (pending) would require treatment works to refuse industrial waste from fracking operations that contain high levels of radium. Waste must be tested for radioactive containments, and the bill would provide for scheduled wastewater discharges.

Well Location Restrictions

A number of states are considering well setbacks or location restrictions to create buffers between drilling and public drinking water resources. In New York, pending A.B. 4237 and S.B. 1230 would prohibit drilling within 10 miles of the New York City water supply infrastructure. A few pending bills in Pennsylvania address well spacing or location restrictions. H.B. 230, for example, would prohibit drilling within the surface or subsurface area of, or using hydraulic fracturing or horizontal drilling within, 2,500 feet of any primary source of a community water system.

Monitoring to Improve Knowledge Base

Water Withdrawal Monitoring

Water quality monitoring may help improve knowledge of how hydraulic fracturing affects water supplies and quality. In New York, pending legislation (S.B. 3483 and A.B. 7986) would require groundwater testing prior to and after drilling wells for oil and gas.

Drilling Moratoria

Some state legislators are aiming to delay hydraulic fracturing operations until more is known about its effects. Michigan's pending H.B. 5150, for example, would prohibit hydraulic fracturing under certain circumstances until a specified advisory committee makes recommendations. New Jersey enacted legislation (S.B. 2576) to impose a one-year moratorium on hydraulic fracturing in order to investigate the potential effects of hydraulic fracturing on air and water quality in the state. In New York, pending A.B. 5547 would establish a moratorium until 120 days after the US EPA issues its report on the effects of a fracking treatment. Most recently, Vermont enacted H.B. 464 to prohibit hydraulic fracturing in the state.

Federal Action

At the federal level, many regulations govern aspects of hydraulic fracturing, such as the disposal of fluid waste deep underground and certain reporting requirements. The Underground Injection Control (UIC) program set forth in the Safe Drinking Water Act "regulates the subsurface emplacement of fluid." However, the Energy Policy act of 2005 provided language to exempt hydraulic fracturing from UIC regulation. Congress has considered legislation—known as the FRAC Act—that would remove this exemption and require public disclosure of chemicals used in fracking treatments.

New Jersey adopted a resolution, and Pennsylvania legislators proposed a resolution, urging Congress to pass the FRAC Act. However, legislators in at least four states—Kansas, North Dakota, South Dakota and Utah—proposed resolutions to urge Congress to limit federal regulation of hydraulic fracturing. North Dakota adopted HCR 3053a, urging Congress to clearly limit US EPA regulation of hydraulic fracturing under the Safe Drinking Water Act to well stimulation treatments that use diesel fuel as the primary constituent of hydraulic fracturing fluid. Utah enacted SCR 12, urging Congress to clearly delegate responsibility for regulating hydraulic fracturing to the states.

In May 2011, Secretary of Energy Chu asked an advisory board subcommittee to make recommendations to improve the safety and environmental performance of hydraulic fracturing. The subcommittee held several public meetings throughout 2011 and released its final report in November 2011.

The report focuses on implementation of 20 recommendations for reducing the environmental impacts of shale gas production. It stresses the importance of using best practices in measurement and public disclosure, improving air quality, protecting water quality and disclosing hydraulic fracturing fluid components.

In February 2012, the US Department of Interior released draft regulations that would require operators on public lands to seek approval to conduct hydraulic fracturing and disclose the chemical ingredients of proposed fracking fluid, but trade secrets are protected. The proposal also would require operators to outline a record-keeping method and would require a mechanical integrity test of the casing prior to well stimulation. The US EPA also is investigating the potential effects of hydraulic fracturing on drinking water resources. Initial study results should be released by the end of 2012, followed by a final report in 2014.

Outlook

Shale gas has transformed the domestic energy outlook. Natural gas development offers significant benefits, and states are working to ensure safe gas extraction, especially in densely populated regions.

In 2012, fracking will continue to be debated. Top legislative trends likely will be in fracking fluid disclosure and monitoring. Many states also will consider how to treat and dispose of waste to protect water sources; improve drill casing and well spacing requirements to prevent spills and leaks; and consider severance tax changes to help environmental projects, mitigate impacts on local communities and balance state budgets.

The Environmental Impact of Natural Gas

Union of Concerned Scientists

The Union of Concerned Scientists puts rigorous, independent science to work to solve our planet's most pressing problems.

Global Warming Emissions

Natural gas is a fossil fuel, though the global warming emissions from its combustion are much lower than those from coal or oil.

Natural gas emits 50 to 60 percent less carbon dioxide (CO_2) when combusted in a new, efficient natural gas power plant compared with emissions from a typical new coal plant. Considering only tailpipe emissions, natural gas also emits 15 to 20 percent less heat-trapping gases than gasoline when burned in today's typical vehicle.

Emissions from smokestacks and tailpipes, however, do not tell the full story.

The drilling and extraction of natural gas from wells and its transportation in pipelines results in the leakage of methane, primary component of natural gas that is 34 times stronger than CO_2 at trapping heat over a 100-year period and 86 times stronger over 20 years. Preliminary studies and field measurements show that these so-called "fugitive" methane emissions range from 1 to 9 percent of total life cycle emissions.

Whether natural gas has lower life cycle greenhouse gas emissions than coal and oil depends on the assumed leakage rate, the global warming potential of methane over different time frames, the energy conversion efficiency, and other factors. One recent study found that methane losses must be kept below 3.2 percent for natural gas power plants to have lower life cycle emissions than new coal plants over short time frames of 20 years or fewer. And if burning natural gas in vehicles is to deliver even marginal benefits,

"Environmental Impacts of Natural Gas," Union of Concerned Scientists. http://www.ucsusa.org/clean-energy/coal-and-other-fossil-fuels/environmental-impacts-of-natural-gas#.Wfw-BbWjfcs. Reprinted by permission.

methane losses must be kept below 1 percent and 1.6 percent compared with diesel fuel and gasoline, respectively. Technologies are available to reduce much of the leaking methane, but deploying such technology would require new policies and investments.

Air Pollution

Cleaner burning than other fossil fuels, the combustion of natural gas produces negligible amounts of sulfur, mercury, and particulates. Burning natural gas does produce nitrogen oxides (NOx), which are precursors to smog, but at lower levels than gasoline and diesel used for motor vehicles. DOE analyses indicate that every 10,000 US homes powered with natural gas instead of coal avoids the annual emissions of 1,900 tons of NO_x, 3,900 tons of SO_2, and 5,200 tons of particulates. Reductions in these emissions translate into public health benefits, as these pollutants have been linked with problems such as asthma, bronchitis, lung cancer, and heart disease for hundreds of thousands of Americans.

However, despite these benefits, unconventional gas development can affect local and regional air quality. Some areas where drilling occurs have experienced increases in concentrations of hazardous air pollutants and two of the six "criteria pollutants"—particulate matter and ozone plus its precursors—regulated by the EPA because of their harmful effects on health and the environment. Exposure to elevated levels of these air pollutants can lead to adverse health outcomes, including respiratory symptoms, cardiovascular disease, and cancer. One recent study found that residents living less than half a mile from unconventional gas well sites were at greater risk of health effects from air pollution from natural gas development than those living farther from the well sites.

Land Use and Wildlife

The construction and land disturbance required for oil and gas drilling can alter land use and harm local ecosystems by causing erosion and fragmenting wildlife habitats and migration patterns.

When oil and gas operators clear a site to build a well pad, pipelines, and access roads, the construction process can cause erosion of dirt, minerals, and other harmful pollutants into nearby streams.

A study of hydraulic fracturing impacts in Michigan found potential environmental impacts to be "significant" and include increased erosion and sedimentation, increased risk of aquatic contamination from chemical spills or equipment runoff, habitat fragmentation, and reduction of surface waters as a result of the lowering of groundwater levels.

Water Use and Pollution

Unconventional oil and gas development may pose health risks to nearby communities through contamination of drinking water sources with hazardous chemicals used in drilling the wellbore, hydraulically fracturing the well, processing and refining the oil or gas, or disposing of wastewater. Naturally occurring radioactive materials, methane, and other underground gases have sometimes leaked into drinking water supplies from improperly cased wells; methane is not associated with acute health effects but in sufficient volumes may pose flammability concerns. The large volumes of water used in unconventional oil and gas development also raise water-availability concerns in some communities.

Groundwater

There have been documented cases of groundwater near oil and gas wells being contaminated with fracking fluids as well as with gases, including methane and volatile organic compounds. One major cause of gas contamination is improperly constructed or failing wells that allow gas to leak from the well into groundwater. Cases of contamination have been documented in Ohio and Pennsylvania.

Another potential avenue for groundwater contamination is natural or man-made fractures in the subsurface, which could allow stray gas to move directly between an oil and gas formation and groundwater supplies.

In addition to gases, groundwater can become contaminated with hydraulic fracturing fluid. In several cases, groundwater was contaminated from surface leaks and spills of fracturing fluid. Fracturing fluid also may migrate along abandoned wells, around improperly sealed and constructed wells, through induced fractures, or through failed wastewater pit liners.

Surface Water

Unconventional oil and gas development also poses contamination risks to surface waters through spills and leaks of chemical additives, spills and leaks of diesel or other fluids from equipment on-site, and leaks of wastewater from facilities for storage, treatment, and disposal. Unlike groundwater contamination risks, surface water contamination risks are mostly related to land management and to on- and off-site chemical and wastewater management.

The EPA has identified more than 1,000 chemical additives that are used for hydraulic fracturing, including acids (notably hydrochloric acid), bactericides, scale removers, and friction-reducing agents. Only maybe a dozen chemicals are used for any given well, but the choice of which chemicals is well-specific, depending on the geochemistry and needs of that well. Large quantities—tens of thousands of gallons for each well—of the chemical additives are trucked to and stored on a well pad. If not managed properly, the chemicals could leak or spill out of faulty storage containers or during transport.

Drilling muds, diesel, and other fluids can also spill at the surface. Improper management of flowback or produced wastewater can cause leaks and spills. There is also risk to surface water from deliberate improper disposal of wastewater by bad actors.

Water Use

The growth of hydraulic fracturing and its use of huge volumes of water per well may strain local ground and surface water supplies, particularly in water-scarce areas. The amount of water used for hydraulically fracturing a well can vary because of differences in formation geology, well construction, and the type of hydraulic fracturing process used. The EPA estimates that 70 billion to 140 billion gallons of water were used nationwide in 2011 for fracturing an estimated 35,000 wells. Unlike other energy-related water withdrawals, which are commonly returned to rivers and lakes, most of the water used for unconventional oil and gas development is not recoverable. Depending on the type of well along with its depth and location, a single well with horizontal drilling can require 3 million to 12 million gallons of water when it is first fractured—dozens of times more than what is used in conventional vertical wells. Similar vast volumes of water are needed each time a well undergoes a "work over," or additional fracturing later in its life to maintain well pressure and gas production. A typical shale gas well will have about two work overs during its productive life span.

Earthquakes

Hydraulic fracturing itself has been linked to low-magnitude seismic activity—less than 2 moment magnitude (M) [the moment magnitude scale now replaces the Richter scale—but such mild events are usually undetectable at the surface. The disposal of fracking wastewater by injecting it at high pressure into deep Class II injection wells, however, has been linked to larger earthquakes in the United States. At least half of the 4.5 M or larger earthquakes to strike the interior of the United States in the past decade have occurred in regions of potential injection-induced seismicity. Although it can be challenging to attribute individual earthquakes to injection, in many cases the association is supported by timing and location of the events.

Engineers Have an Ethical Responsibility When Evaluating Fracking Risk

Robert Kirkman, Chloé F. Arson, Lauren Stewart,
Rebecca Harris, Amanda Francis

Dr. Robert Kirkman is an associate professor in the School of Public Policy at the Georgia Institute of Technology. Arson, Stewart, Harris, and Francis studied and conducted research at the School of Civil and Environmental Engineering at the Georgia Institute of Technology.

O ne third of US natural gas is extracted by injecting fluid at high pressure into shale formations, a process associated with a number of possible hazards and risks that have become the subject of intense public controversy. We develop a three-part schema to make sense of risks of hydraulic fracturing and the responsibilities of engineers: the lab, the field, and the forum. In the lab, researchers seek to answer basic questions about, for example, the behavior of shale under particular conditions; there uncertainty seems to arise at every turn. In the field, engineers and others work to implement technological processes, such as hydraulic fracturing and the subsequent extraction of oil and gas; hazards may arise as natural and social systems respond in sometimes surprising ways. In the forum, the public and their representatives deliberate about risk and acceptable risk, questions that are framed in ethical as well as technical terms. The difficulty of characterizing—and in living up to—the responsibilities of engineers lie in part in the apparent distance between the lab and the forum. We examine in turn uncertainties in the lab, hazards in the field, and deliberation in the forum, leading to the conclusion that scientists and engineers can and should help to inform public deliberation but that their research cannot, on its own, resolve all controversies. Scientists

Kirkman R, Arson CF, Stewart L, Harris R, Francis A. The risks of hydraulic fracturing and the responsibilities of engineers. Elem Sci Anth. 2017;5:17. DOI: http://doi.org/10.1525/elementa.218

and engineers who seek to inform deliberation should be mindful of the scope and limits of their authority, clear and modest in communicating research findings to the public, and careful to avoid even apparent conflicts of interest wherever possible. We close by drawing from the lab-field-forum schema to suggest a direction for pedagogical innovations aimed at the formation of responsible engineers in the context of college-level degree programs.

Introduction

In the autumn of 2013, two of the faculty authors met informally to talk over matters of common interest. This is not so unusual, except that one is an engineer specializing in geomechanics and the other a philosopher specializing in practical ethics. The common interest, though, was in understanding the ethical responsibilities of scientists and engineers and, perhaps more importantly, in developing new approaches of integrating ethics instruction into engineering curricula.

That initial conversation led to a collaboration that drew in the other authors of this paper—another faculty member in engineering and two (then) undergraduate students—as well as a graduate student and a librarian. The aim of the collaboration was to grapple with the risks of hydraulic fracturing—and of unconventional oil and gas exploitation more generally—and the concomitant responsibilities of scientists and engineers.

[...]

A basic premise of our entire project is that scientific and engineering research does have a vital role in deliberation on public policy regarding hydraulic fracturing. Indeed, it is difficult to imagine a legitimate and informed policy process that somehow excludes the work and the voices of engineers and scientists! Theirs are not the only voices that matter, however, and in that fact lie a number of their responsibilities in the forum.

We should also briefly clarify the meanings of some basic terms we have already been using: uncertainty, hazard, harm and risk.

Hydraulic fracturing and the subsequent extraction of gas and oil involve *risk*. In empirical terms, risk is the product of two factors: *hazard* and *harm*. Hazard is variability in how the environment responds to a particular intervention expressed as the probability of some adverse occurrence. Harm is the degree to which individuals affected by the adverse occurrence are made worse off in some substantive way, whether in terms of personal wellbeing, security, or property, or as a decrease in net utility, sometimes expressed in monetary terms.

Uncertainty adds further complexity to understanding risk, in that the probability of a given hazard and the magnitude of the resulting harm often cannot be specified due to insufficient understanding of the underlying dynamics.

To restate the purpose of this paper, then, we consider how and to what extent engineers and scientists can address *uncertainty*, specify *hazards* and respond to *risks* in the practice of hydraulic fracturing, and what might be their appropriate contributions to public deliberation concerning *acceptable risk*—a term about which we have more to say below.

In the Field: Identifying Hazards

The careful work of researchers outlined above can provide insight into just one piece of the larger puzzle. Hydraulic fracturing and the extraction of oil and gas also involve other systems at other scales, modeled by researchers in other fields. Accordingly, we turn now to an overview of some of the main hazards associated with hydraulic fracturing, drawing from various sources. The focus is not so much on the modeling of basic dynamics as on the probability of adverse outcomes as experienced by people and other living beings.

In terms of our schema, we are leaving the lab on the way to the forum, taking in the various ways in which the mechanics and dynamics of hydraulic fracturing and subsequent resource extraction may become matters of public concern in the field.

Induced Seismicity

One hazard often associated with hydraulic fracturing in the public imagination are earthquakes caused by the injection of fluid into shale beds. The magnitude (M) of an earthquake indicates the quantity of energy liberated by the seismic source. For an event to be felt, the magnitude needs to exceed 2 (M >2). In the US, seismic events that are likely related to energy development have been documented in Alabama, Arkansas, California, Colorado, Illinois, Louisiana, Mississippi, Nebraska, Nevada, New Mexico, Ohio, Oklahoma and Texas.

Criteria used by the scientific community to establish correlations between seismic events and human activity include "the amplitude and direction of the state of stress in the Earth's crust in the vicinity of the fluid injection or withdrawal area; the presence, orientation, and physical properties of nearby faults; pore fluid pressure (pressure of fluids in the pores of the rocks at depth, hereafter simply called pore pressure); pore pressure change; the rates and volumes of fluid being injected or withdrawn; and the rock properties in the subsurface" (National Research Council, 2013).

The lack of data (pre- and post-event, near and far from the energy exploitation site) often impedes the establishment of a causal link between a particular seismic event and human activity. The National Research Council (2013) reported that earthquakes attributed to energy geotechnologies are caused by a change in pore pressure and/or stress in the presence of faults (with specific properties and orientation) and critical states of stress in situ. Statistical analysis found that the closer to zero the net fluid balance (total balance of fluid injected into or removed from the subsurface), the less seismicity is induced.

As of 2013, only one case of felt seismicity (M ~ 2.8) in the US was linked with high probability to hydraulic fracturing for shale gas development, out of 35,000 hydraulically fractured shale gas wells. The National Research Council (2013) explained this low number was caused by the short time of injection and small volume of liquid injected in the process of hydraulic fracturing in shale reservoirs. In general, the seismic events are too small, the regional networks are too sparse, and the data quality is often too poor to confirm a causal link to fluid injection for energy development.

That said, causal links have been established between the injection wells used for wastewater from hydraulic fracturing operations (over 150,000 wells in the U.S) and previously unrecognized faults in the subsurface. Although most disposal wells involve injection of wastewater at low pressure into aquifers of high porosity and permeability, the long-term effects of the increasing number of injection wells remain unknown.

In 2014, researchers at the US Geological Survey studied a human-induced M5.0 earthquake near Prague, Oklahoma, which occurred in November 2011. The M5.0 foreshock occurred in close proximity to active fluid injection wells. The fluid injection caused a buildup of pore fluid pressure, and a decrease in the fault strength causing rupture (Sumy et al., 2014). The research, which analyzes the role of coseismic stress transfer along the fault, also suggests that the foreshock may have triggered the M5.7 mainshock, which in turn triggered thousands of aftershocks along separate portions of the Wilzetta fault system, including a M5.0 aftershock. If this hypothesis is correct, the M5.7 earthquake in Prague, Oklahoma would be the largest and most powerful earthquake ever associated with wastewater injection to date.

More current research has developed various techniques to demonstrate the probable connections between hydraulic fracturing and the various seismic events around the country. For example, in a study published in 2015, an optimized multi-station cross-correlation template-matching routine identified 77 events in Poland Township, Ohio, which coincided with nearby hydraulic fracturing operations and had local magnitudes (M_L) of up to 3. These earthquakes were some of the largest induced by hydraulic fracturing in the United States (Skoumal et al., 2015).

In summary, the mechanisms that cause earthquakes are known and the relationships among hydraulic fracturing, wastewater injection wells, and seismic activity have been determined and refined through ongoing research, but scientists cannot predict their occurrence, because (1) there is insufficient data on fault locations and properties, in situ stresses, fluid pressures, and rock properties; and (2) current modeling tools do not account for all the thermo-hydro-chemo-mechanical processes that take place in fractured rock systems.

Fresh Water Consumption

Another matter of public concern is that hydraulic fracturing may draw from local supplies of fresh water as a base for fracturing fluid. In some regions, this may raise the possibility of shortages of fresh water for other uses.

In fact, the volume of water injected for hydraulic fracturing is highly dependent on the type of geologic formation, the depth of the formation and the length of well exploited (including the horizontal part of the well). So-called low-volume hydraulic fracturing, typically conducted in vertical wells, requires between 20,000 and 80,000 gallons of water or other fluid. By contrast, high-volume hydraulic fracturing in low permeability formations such as shales often include long horizontal well segments and require millions of gallons of water: 3 to more than 5 million gallons per well in Marcellus shale and up to 7.8 million gallons for a multi-stage fracturing operation in a horizontal well (Environmental Protection Agency, 2015). Greater demand for fresh water in some shale gas producing counties raises concerns about the impact on the local ecosystem, particularly from short term, high volume withdrawals. Moreover, the overall assessment of the exploitation of water resources is complicated by some vocabulary inconsistencies, illustrated by the following excerpt: "It is not known whether any of [the disclosures reported in FracFocus 1.0] used the term 'fresh' to refer to recycled fluids that was [sic.] treated to achieve the quality of fresh water. [...] Differences observed among disclosures from different states are likely due, in part, to variations in the rate of overall reporting of water sources and inconsistencies in terminology used" (Environmental Protection Agency, 2015).

The newest hydraulic fracturing technologies are based on the injection of gels instead of freshwater-based fluids. Still, there is increasing concern about potential local or regional water shortages that could occur if the number of injection wells continues to grow. The volumetric recovery of injected water depends on the mineral composition and microstructure of shale, and varies over the life span of a well. Reported recovery rates range between 5% and 85%. As of 2012, companies were recycling 14% of hydraulic fracturing wastewater (i.e., using it again for further hydraulic fracturing), up from 1% in 2010. In 2014, representative recovery rates were estimated to lie between 30% and 50% (Stringfellow et al., 2014). Further, recent changes at the state government level have shown the potential to reduce regulation and encourage wastewater recycling. For example, in March 2015, the New Mexico Oil Conservation Commission published a rule to encourage oil and gas producers to recycle wastewater by reducing wastewater storage requirements in recycling facilities (Small, 2015).

[…]

Explosion Hazards

There have been explosive events associated with hydraulic fracturing. The explosive hazard is located, not deep underground, but on and just below the surface: it is most often related to storage of hydraulic fracturing fluids in pressure vessels and to flaws in the design, construction and maintenance of the machinery on the surface, including the wellhead itself.

For example, on the morning of February 11, 2014, a large gas well explosion and fire in Dunkard Township, Pennsylvania, was reported to the Pennsylvania Emergency Management Agency (PEMA). The explosion killed one worker and injured another, and the subsequent fire spread to an adjacent well, which in turn triggered the explosion of a propane tanker truck on the site. In all, it took emergency personnel over 12 hours to extinguish the flames (Department of Environmental Protection (PA), 2014).

After the event, the Pennsylvania Department of Environmental Protection (DEP) conducted a thorough investigation, which concluded that the explosion originated from natural gas leaking from the wellhead under high pressure. The gland nut and lockscrews, used in wellhead equipment to mechanically energize or retain internal wellhead components, were ejected from the machinery, suggesting a possible cause. Apparently, the assembly on the wellhead was loosened several days before this incident and was not properly re-secured. The DEP provided a set of recommendations to the well owner to prevent future incidents. These recommendations include inspection and quality control issues for the gland nut and lockscrew mechanisms. The recommendations put the responsibility to prevent future explosions on the well owners, inspectors, contractors and engineers associated with the well (Colaneri, 2014).

[...]

The Responsibilities of Engineers

Having examined some of the particular uncertainties, hazards and risks of hydraulic fracturing, and briefly addressed some of the values involved in acceptable risk, we return to our initial question: What are the responsibilities of engineers and scientists in addressing risk and uncertainty, and participating in public deliberation regarding hydraulic fracturing?

We said at the outset that the two frames of reference—the lab and the forum—are so distinct from one another as to seem unconnected, especially in regards to the scales and terms of inquiry that predominate in each. The example of hydraulic fracturing suggests, however, that the lab and the forum are connected at least in one direction: the work of the forum in deliberating about the risks associated with engineered systems requires the direct contributions of researchers and engineers whose main work is in the lab or in the field.

There is also a connection in the other direction, to the extent researchers and engineers are *professionals*. To be a professional is to hold a particular status and prestige, granted by the public and held in trust to the public. So, to be a researcher or an engineer, in the lab or in the field, is already to play a defined social role, one sanctioned and supported by the forum.

We emphasize this is a delimited role, including bounds to the scope of professional authority: in general, professionals are prohibited from offering professional judgment on matters beyond their particular expertise. A doctor offering an expert opinion on a matter of law, or a civil engineer on a matter of chemical engineering, would be overstepping that limit and so breaking the public trust. This leads us to suggest three, relatively modest obligations on scientists and engineers in their relationship to the public forum.

First, engineers and scientists in their role as experts seeking to inform public deliberation ought to remain within the limitations of that role. They may have authority on the answers to particular empirical questions, but not over every question of policy. In other words, researchers ought to keep in mind that sound empirical research in the lab and sound technical judgment in the field may be necessary for good policy, but they are not sufficient as a basis for good policy in the forum.

Second, engineers and scientists ought to exercise due modesty in reporting the results of empirical research, making the scope and limits of each finding and model as clear as possible. This includes acknowledging and describing remaining areas of uncertainty, especially those that may be most relevant to questions of public interest.

Third, engineers and scientists in their role as experts seeking to inform public deliberation should be careful of apparent, potential and actual conflict of interest, and they should beware of the risk of capture by parties with vested interests in particular policy outcomes. They ought to avoid even apparent conflicts of interest whenever possible, and they ought to disclose those conflicts where they are unavoidable.

[…]

Fracking's Environmental Impacts: Water

Greenpeace

Greenpeace is an independent global campaigning organization that acts to change attitudes and behavior, to protect and conserve the environment, and to promote peace.

In order to frack, an enormous amount of water is mixed with various toxic chemical compounds to create frack fluid. This frack fluid is further contaminated by the heavy metals and radioactive elements that exist naturally in the shale. A significant portion of the frack fluid returns to the surface, where it can spill or be dumped into rivers and streams. Underground water supplies can also be contaminated by fracking, through migration of gas and frack fluid underground.

Water Use

In order to hydraulically fracture shale and extract the hydrocarbons, large quantities of water and chemicals must be injected underground. Thus frackingcan pose a threat to local water resources, especially in areas where water is already scarce like the Barnett shale in Texas. In the Marcellus Shale region, the most expansive shale play in the United States, 2 to 10 million gallons of water are needed every time a well is fractured. Because wells can be fractured multiple times, the total amount of water used for fracking is unknown and can vary by location and technology. In western states like Texas and Colorado, over 3.6 million gallons are needed per fracture. In 2010, the US EPA estimated that 70 to 140 billion gallons of water were used to fracture just 35,000 wells in the United States, more than was used by the city of Denver, Colorado in the same time period. As of 2012, the fracking industry has drilled around 1.2 million wells, and is slated to add at least 35,000 new wells every year.

"Fracking's Environmental Impacts: Water," Greenpeace USA, Reprinted by permission.

(Jeff Goodell, "The Big Fracking Bubble: The Scam Behind the Gas Boom," *Rolling Stone* 3/12/12)

Because of the cost to truck water in from further away, companies prefer to use water from sources as close to the well as possible, which can result in significant impacts on local waterways and overburden local water treatment facilities. In Texas, which is suffering dangerous drought conditions, fracking continues even as water use by citizens is restricted, the landscape wilts and the animal life dies. In 2011 the *Wall Street Journal* reported that the diversion of water for fracking oil and gas wells is also a serious threat to ranchers and other businesses in Texas. (Russell Gold and Ana Campoy, "Oil's Growing Thirst for Water," *Wall Street Journal*, 12/6/2011)

Storage Impacts

Because of the tremendous amount of water needed for hydraulic fracturing, fresh water must be acquired, transported, and stored for every well pad. To manage the massive amounts of water necessary for the hydraulic fracturing process, drillers build large open air pits called impoundments next to the well pads, to store the water before it is used and after it returns to the surface.

There are two types of impoundments, those that hold drilling waste, used while drilling the well bore, and impoundments for the fracking fluid. The frack fluid pits are larger and contain toxic fracking fluid. These open pits have been linked to animal deaths and health effects in humans. In Texas, which has few laws regarding wastewater disposal, there is no requirement to line the pits to prevent seepage.

Fracking Fluids: A Toxic Brew

During the hydraulic fracturing of a well, water is mixed with various chemicals to make a toxic brew called frack fluid. Until recently, neither the federal nor state governments required drilling companies to disclose the ingredients used in frack fluids. Some states have begun to require that companies disclose the chemicals they use, but even in such cases, companies can withhold some chemical names under trade secret exemptions. As a result, a comprehensive list of chemicals used in the fracking process does not exist. Some states have begun to require that companies disclose the chemicals they use, but even in such cases, confidential business information claims result in only partial disclosures. Corporations involved in fracking, like ExxonMobil, have inserted loopholes in drilling legislation that allow them to keep various chemicals used in the fracking process secret.

Some companies have disclosed the contents of their frack fluid in response to community concerns and congressional pressure. In April 2011, an industry group known as the Interstate Oil and Gas Compact Commission launched www.fracfocus.org, a web-based disclosure database for wells drilled after 2010. In addition, a Congressional investigation found that between 2005 and 2009 oil and gas service companies used 29 different chemicals in their fracking fluid known to cause cancer or other health risks. (House Energy and Commerce Committee, "Chemicals Used in Hydraulic Fracturing," April, 2011)

Gas companies routinely claim that frack fluid is harmless because the concentration of chemical additives is low, about two percent. But just 2% of the billions of gallons of frack fluid created by gas drillers measures up to the use of hundreds of tons of toxic chemicals. A 2011 report to Congress estimated that from 2005 to 2009, 14 leading fracking companies used (before mixing with water) 780 million gallons of 750 different chemicals. (House Energy and Commerce Committee, Minority Staff Report, "Chemicals Used in Hydraulic Fracturing," April, 2011)

Drilling wastewater is so poisonous, when a gas company that legally doused a patch of West Virginia forest with salty wastewater from a drilling operation, it killed ground vegetation within days and more than half the trees within two years. Wastewater from fracking has also been linked to livestock and family pet deaths across the country.

Moreover, many chemicals used in fracking have been

documented to have deleterious health effects at small levels of exposure.

Some of the chemicals that comprise frack fluid are highly toxic and cancer causing, like Benzene, Toluene, 2-butoxyethanol (a main ingredient to anti-freeze and oil dispersants), and heavy metals. The Endocrine Disruptor Exchange (TEDX) identified 353 chemicals used in fracking, many of which can cause cancer and other serious health, even in small doses.

Once the frack fluid mixture is injected into the ground it can also pick up or entrain further contaminants, like radium, a cancer-causing radioactive particle found deep within the Marcellus and other shales. Radium has a half life of over 1,000 years and is produced from Uranium, which has a much longer half life. Because Radium is water soluble, all frack fluid used in the Marcellus Shalebecomes radioactive to some degree.

Contamination of Water Wells and Gas Migration

One of the gravest threats posed by fracking is the contamination of drinking water wells, vital sources of water for many rural communities. Though the industry has attempted to obscure evidence of well water contamination by fracking, multiple instances have come to light.

- In Pennsylvania, Colorado, Ohio and Wyoming, fracking has been linked to drinking water contamination and property damage.
- A Duke study examining 60 sites in New York and Pennsylvania found "systematic evidence for methane contamination" in household drinking water. Water wells half a mile from drilling operations were contaminated by methane at 17 times the rate of those farther from gas developments. Although methane in water has not been studied closely as a health hazard, it can seep into houses and build up to explosive levels.
- In December 2011, US EPA released a 121-page draft report linking the contamination of drinking water wells near the town of Pavillion, Wyoming to nearby gas drilling.

- An investigation by ProPublica found that years after their wells were contaminated by nearby fracking operations, EPA began to supply water to residents of Dimock, Pennsylvania.
- In New York, claims have already been filed against the Anschutz Exploration Corporation and its subcontractors on behalf of nine families for the contamination of their drinking water due to natural gas exploration and drilling.
- A scene in "Gasland," a documentary in which a homeowner was able to light the water flowing out of his kitchen tap, made many people aware of the dangers of fracking. Scientific American also published a ProPublica investigation that found "a string of documented cases of gas escaping into drinking water—in Pennsylvania and other states."
- A 1987 report concluded that hydraulic fracturing fluids or gel used by the Kaiser Exploration and Mining Company contaminated a well roughly 600 feet away on the property of James Parsons in Jackson County, W.Va.

In spite of the evidence, the oil and gas industry routinely claims that fracking has never resulted in water contamination.

How Fracking Contaminates

Groundwater becomes contaminated by hydraulic fracturing in a number of ways, including leakage from liquid storage areas, leakage from injection wells, leakage during hydrofracking along faults or up abandoned wells, seepage into the ground when wastewater and residuals are applied to land (i.e. used for irrigation or on roads for dust suppression or de-icing), and other means. (US EPA, Science Advisory Board, Hydraulic Fracturing Review Panel, report to Lisa P. Jackson, August 4, 2011).

The cement casing which rings the well bore and goes through underground aquifers is meant to act as a barrier between underground water and the shaft through which frack fluid and gas flow. But the casing can fail or break during the fracturing process, allowing the frack fluid or naturally-occurring contaminants to contaminate groundwater. When that happens, frack fluid and methane can leak from the well bore directly into the water supply, causing dangerous gas buildups, and making water unfit to drink. (Abrahm Lustgarten and ProPublica, "Drill for Natural Gas, Pollute Water," *Scientific American*, 11/17/2008)

Even if the cement casings hold, gas can travel up from the shale layer to the water table. When gas travels through fractures in the rock layer above the shale and in to water supplies, it is called gas migration. (Abrahm Lustgarten and ProPublica, "Does Natural Gas Make Water Burn?" *Scientific American*, 4/27/09)

It is common for wells to lose pressure during the fracking stage, which indicates that the frack fluid is not contained within the well and is seeping into some place the drillers did not anticipate. There has not been enough study of this phenomenon, even though drillers indicate it happens on a frequent basis.

Frack Fluid Disposal

Disposal of the toxic and sometimes radioactive frack fluid is a major logistical problem for fracking companies. When a well is hydraulically fractured, somewhere between 18 and 80 percent of the frack fluid injected into the well will return to the surface. This water, called "flowback" is heavily contaminated by the chemical mixtures that comprise the frack fluid, as well as dissolved salts and heavy metals from deep within the earth. Estimates from the industry indicate that drillers in Pennsylvania created approximately 19 million gallons of this wastewater per day in 2011. The Susquehanna River Basin Commission estimates 20 million gallons per day (MGD) for that same timeframe. ("Permitting Strategy for High Total Dissolved Solids Wastewater Discharges,"4/11/2009) There is currently no comprehensive set of national standards for the disposal of fracking wastewater (see "Halliburton Loophole").

The presence of certain contaminants commonly found in fracking wastewater—including bromide (which can create toxic by-products) and radionuclides, as well as Total Dissolved Solids (TDS) like salts (for which conventional wastewater treatment is largely ineffective)—are of major concern not only because of the potential impacts on rivers, streams and groundwater, but also for downstream water treatment plants, where conventional treatment technologies are not equipped to deal with such contaminants. According to US EPA, "only a limited number of Publicly Owned Treatment Plants (POTWs) have the ancillary treatment technologies needed to remove the constituents in hydraulic fracturing return waters." (US EPA, Science Advisory Board, Hydraulic Fracturing Review Panel, report to Lisa P. Jackson, August 4, 2011)

Because of lax regulation, fracking companies commonly dispose of contaminated fracking water in the cheapest, easiest ways they can find, regardless of the consequences for communities, water treatment facilities, and the environment. This has led to abuses of waterways and communities close to frack sites.

The New York Times reported that in Pennsylvania, wastewater contaminated with radium and other carcinogens was dumped upstream from the intake pipe of a drinking water plant. (Ian Urbina, "Regulation Lax as Gas Wells' Tainted Water Hits Rivers," *New York Times*, 2/26/2011)

Often, wastewater is stored in large evaporation pits, which can off-gas volatile chemicals. Off-gassing is the evaporation of volatile chemicals at normal atmospheric pressure. In 2008, scientists recorded high levels of Volatile Organic Compounds (VOCs) from gas production operations in Colorado, and high levels of wintertime ozone pollution have been linked to oil and gas operations in Wyoming and Utah. (Guyathri Vaidyanathan, "Colo. Plan goes after haze tied to oil and gas operations," E&E Reporter, 3/12/2012; Mark Jaffe, "Like Wyoming, Utah finds high level of wintertime ozone pollution near oil, gas wells," *Denver Post*, 2/26/2012)

The solid waste left over from evaporation pits and land application is treated as ordinary solid waste and exempt from many federal and state regulations, though it can contain toxic residue from the frack fluid. (Ian Urbina, "Recycling of fracking wastewater is no cure-all," *New York Times*, 2/2/2011) Drillers are permitted to apply fracking wastewater residues to roads for de-icing and dust suppression in states like Pennsylvania and New York, and allowed to spray it into the air over tracks of land used for agriculture in Texas.

EPA's Study of Hydraulic Fracturing Impacts on Groundwater

In 2015, a Greenpeace investigation found that the shale industry had undue influence on EPA's study of fracking's impact on groundwater.

Organizations to Contact

The editors have compiled the following list of organizations concerned with the issues debated in this book. The descriptions are derived from materials provided by the organizations. All have publications or information available for interested readers. This list was compiled on the date of publication of the present volume; the information provided here may change. Be aware that many organizations take several weeks or longer to respond to inquiries, so allow as much time as possible.

American Coal Foundation (ACF)
101 Constitution Avenue, NW
Suite 500 East
Washington, DC 20001-2133
phone: (202) 463-9785
email: info@teachcoal.org
website: teachcoal.org

The American Coal Foundation provides students and teachers with educational materials related to coal. The ACF offers free lesson plans to help educators teach about energy. In addition, the ACF shares information about energy conservation, coal mining, and much more.

American Council on Renewable Energy (ACORE)
PO Box 33518
Washington, DC 20033
phone: (202) 393-0001
email: info@acore.org
website: www.acore.org

American Council on Renewable Energy is a national nonprofit organization dedicated to advancing the renewable energy sector through market development, policy changes, and financial innovation.

The American Nuclear Society (ANS)

555 North Kensington Avenue
La Grange Park, IL 60526
phone: (800) 323-3044
website: www.ans.org

The American Nuclear Society is a not-for-profit international scientific and educational organization. It was established by a group of individuals who recognized the need to unify the professional activities within the various fields of nuclear science and technology.

American Wind Energy Association (AWEA)

1501 M St. NW, Suite 900
Washington, DC 20005
phone: (202) 383-2500
website: www.awea.org

The American Wind Energy Association (AWEA) is the premier national trade association that represents the interests of America's wind energy industry.

Earth Justice

50 California Street, Suite 500
San Francisco, CA 94111
phone: (800) 584-6460
email: headquarters@earthjustice.org
website: earthjustice.org

As the nation's original and largest nonprofit environmental law organization, Earth Justice leverages expertise and commitment to fight for justice and advance the promise of a healthy world for all.

Energy In Depth

1201 15th Street NW, Suite 300
Washington, DC 20005
phone: (202) 346-8806
email: seth@energyindepth.org
website: energyindepth.org

Launched by the Independent Petroleum Association of America (IPAA) in 2009, Energy In Depth (EID) is a research, education, and public outreach campaign focused on providing information about the potential of responsibly developing America's onshore energy resource base—especially abundant sources of oil and natural gas from shale and other "tight" formations across the country.

Solar Energy Industries Association (SEIA®)

600 14th Street, NW, Suite 400
Washington, DC 20005
phone: (202) 682-0556
email: info@seia.org
website: www.seia.org

The Solar Energy Industries Association is the driving force behind solar energy and is building a strong solar industry to power America through advocacy and education.

The Oil Drum

email: editors@theoildrum.com
website: www.theoildrum.com

A web-based/interactive news site on energy, peak oil, and sustainability research hosted by the nonprofit 501c3 Institute for the Study of Energy and Our Future.

Women of Renewable Industries and Sustainable Energy
(WRISE)
155 Water Street
Brooklyn, NY 11201
phone: (718) 260-9550
website: wrisenergy.org
email: info@wrisenergy.org

Women of Renewable Industries and Sustainable Energy (WRISE) is a national nonprofit with a growing presence working across the renewable energy economy. Its goal is to change the energy future through the actions of women. WRISE works to recruit, retain, and advance women and inspire its members and the public to unite in raising their voices for others.

Bibliography

Books

John Allen. *Careers in Environmental and Energy Technology* (High-Tech Careers). San Diego, CA: Reference Point Press, 2017.

Gretchen Bakke. *The Grid: The Fraying Wires Between Americans and Our Energy Future*. New York, NY: Bloomsbury Publishing, 2016.

Adam Briggle. *A Field Philosopher's Guide to Fracking: How One Texas Town Stood Up to Big Oil and Gas*. New York, NY: W. W. Norton & Company, 2015.

Lester R. Brown. *The Great Transition: Shifting from Fossil Fuels to Solar and Wind Energy*. New York, NY: W. W. Norton & Company, 2015.

Anne C. Cunningham. *Critical Perspectives on Fossil Fuels vs. Renewable Energy* (Analyzing the Issues). New York, NY: Enslow Publishers, Incorporated, 2016.

Barbara Freese. *Coal: A Human History*. New York, NY: Basic Books, 2016.

Russell Gold. *The Boom: How Fracking Ignited the American Energy Revolution and Changed the World*. New York, NY: Simon and Schuster, 2015.

Margaret J. Goldstein. *Fuel Under Fire: Petroleum and Its Perils*. Minneapolis, MN: Lerner Publishing Group, 2015.

Richard Heinberg and David Fridley. *Our Renewable Future: Laying the Path for One Hundred Percent Clean Energy*. Washington, DC: Island Press, 2016.

Sherri Mabry-Gordon. *Out of Gas: Using Up Fossil Fuels* (The End of Life As We Know It). New York, NY: Enslow Publishers, 2016.

Michael E. Mackay. *Solar Energy: An Introduction*. Oxford, United Kingdom: Oxford University Press, 2015.

Richard Martin. *Coal Wars: The Future of Energy and the Fate of the Planet*. New York, NY: St. Martin's Press, 2015.

Wolfgang C. Müller and Paul W. Thurner. *The Politics of Nuclear Energy in Western Europe*. Oxford, United Kingdom: Oxford University Press, 2017.

Meghan L. O'Sullivan. *Windfall: How the New Energy Abundance Upends Global Politics and Strengthens America's Power*. New York, NY: Simon and Schuster, 2017.

Tony Seba. *Clean Disruption of Energy and Transportation: How Silicon Valley Will Make Oil, Nuclear, Natural Gas, Coal, Electric Utilities and Conventional Cars Obsolete by 2030*. Stanford, CA: Tony Seba, 2014.

Periodicals and Internet Sources

Jude Clemente. "Natural Gas Is The Flexibility Needed for More Wind and Solar." *Forbes*, December 31, 2017. https://www.forbes.com.

Emma Dietz. "Going Green in 2017: The Business Case for Renewable Energy." Environmental and Energy Study Institute, February 1, 2017. http://www.eesi.org/articles/view/going-green-in-2017-the-case-for-renewable-energy.

Douglas Ernst. "Obama Admin Regulation Allows Wind Turbines to Kill up to 4,200 Bald Eagles per Company." *Washington Post*, December 14, 2016. https://www.washingtontimes.com/news/2016/dec/14/obama-admin-regulation-allows-wind-turbines-kill-4/.

Mary Beth Griggs. "Why Can't We Decide What to Do About Nuclear Energy? Build Them Up? Or Tear Them Down?" January 8, 2018. https://www.popsci.com/what-to-do-about-nuclear-energy.

Jacqueline Hernandez. "Methane Mystery: Fossil Fuels Spewing Less Methane, but Gas Continues to Accumulate." *Mongabay*, May 15, 2017. https://news.mongabay .com/2017/05/methane-mystery-fossil-fuels-spewing-less -methane-but-gas-continues-to-accumulate/.

Clifford Kraussdec. "Rising Coal Exports Give Short-Term Aid to an Ailing Industry." *New York Times,* December 13, 2017. https://www.nytimes.com/2017/12/13/business/energy -environment/coal-exports.html.

Richard Martin. "Germany Runs Up Against the Limits of Renewables." *MIT Technology Review*, May 24, 2016. https:// www.technologyreview.com/s/601514/germany-runs-up -against-the-limits-of-renewables/.

US Energy Information Administration. "Electricity Explained: Use of Electricity." May 22, 107. https://www.eia.gov/ energyexplained.

US Energy Information Administration. "Nonrenewable Explained." February 9, 2017. https://www.eia.gov/ energyexplained/index.cfm?page=nonrenewable_home.

US Energy Information Administration. "US Energy Facts Explained: Consumption and Production." May 19, 2017. https://www.eia.gov/energyexplained.

US Energy Information Administration. "Renewable Energy Explained." June 1, 2017. https://www.eia.gov/ energyexplained/index.cfm?page=renewable_home.

Index